Tinseltown in the Brain

Tinseltown in the Brain

A whimsical wander through Glasgow in the eighties

DONALD McLAUGHLIN

Catterglen Publishing

First published in 2026

Typeset in Palatino Linotype 12pt

Cover design by Donald McLaughlin
Main image courtesy of *The Print Bay* (on Etsy)

Chapter illustration designs by Donald McLaughlin
(images generated using ChatGPT)

Paperback ISBN: 978-1-9194858-0-5
Hardcover ISBN: 978-1-9194858-1-2
eBook ISBN: 978-1-9194858-2-9

To My Wife

(Who would prefer to remain anonymous)

CONTENTS

	Introduction	3
	Play the Game	5
1	Pop of the Scots	9
2	Clatty Pats	27
3	Tinseltown in the Sun	43
4	Strictly Fun Dancing	57
5	Barra	67
6	Karaoke / Karajokie	77
7	The Three Captains	87
8	The Union	103
9	Scottish Movie Magic	125
10	A Fan of the Scran	137
11	Arran	151
12	Tongs Ya Bass	163

13	The Norwegians	175
14	Sweet Dreams (Are Made of This)	187
15	Hogmanay High Jinks	203
16	Getting Old	215
	After Words	225
	Acknowledgements	227
	Appendix: The Songs	231

INTRODUCTION

Tinseltown in the Rain is one of the defining songs of the 80s. *The Blue Nile*'s 1984 ode to Glasgow perfectly captures the soundtrack of the city.

> *"All men and women. Here we are.*
> *Caught up in this big rhythm."*

Everything about the song is unmistakably eighties, but it's also unmistakably Glasgow. It's nostalgic, understated and melancholic but at the same time sophisticated and atmospheric. Paul Buchanan has described *Tinseltown* as a metaphor for whatever our dreams were. Whatever we've lost.

The track manages to recreate the distinctive feeling of being in a city and is a stunning example of what can be achieved with meticulous production skills and a voice like a Glaswegian Frank Sinatra.

Our memories are often triggered by the music of the time. When I hear an 80s song I think of a rainy Glasgow but with an overwhelming sense of warmth and contentment.

So this memoir is a dry, tongue-in-cheek trip through Scotland's biggest city during what was an unforgettable decade for music. The sights & sounds, the venues, the fashion, the people, the culture and the banter.

Hope you enjoy it!

PLAY THE GAME

You might spot a few eighties song titles popping up here and there. In fact the book is positively littered with them! Some of them jump up and slap you in the face while others lurk a little bit deeper in the narrative. There are **170** in total.

Hopefully you can have a bit of fun spotting them without having to resort to hunting high and low. And as this is a work of non-fiction, everything in here is completely true.

A DISCLAIMER

Although this is essentially a book about the eighties, there will be some inevitable seepage into both the 70s and 90s. I hope that's ok. To be fair, the lines can be a bit blurry at either end of a decade and it feels a bit daft to interrupt the flow.

ANOTHER DISCLAIMER

If you have an intolerance to terrible puns then please *STOP READING IMMEDIATELY* to protect yourself from any further *pun*-ishment. You can always regift the book to someone you don't like.

DEFINITELY THE LAST DISCLAIMER

These disclaimers should not be confused with *The Proclaimers* who are legendary pop-rock twins from Auchtermuchty.

Pop of the Scots
TENNENT'S
T
LAGER

CHAPTER ONE

POP OF THE SCOTS

We always suspected it at the time but it's extremely reassuring to hear your kids tell you that the 1980s was the best decade for music. It absolutely was. Especially if you were Scottish. We had a simply amazing amount of chart topping talent during what was without doubt the golden era for Scot Pop. The list seemed endless…

Simple Minds, Deacon Blue, Altered Images, Ultravox, Orange Juice, The Bluebells, Aztec Camera, Hue & Cry, The Associates, Hipsway, The Blue Nile, Fiction Factory, Lloyd Cole & the Commotions, Del Amitri, Big Country,

The Cocteau Twins, Goodbye Mr McKenzie, Texas, The Jesus & Mary Chain, The Big Dish, Love & Money, The Waterboys, Friends Again, Danny Wilson, Wet Wet Wet, Strawberry Switchblade, Fairground Attraction and *The Proclaimers.*

...and many, many more (as *K-Tel* used to say).

The large majority of these were Glasgow based artists which is a pretty staggering proportion. We can also legitimately claim the *Eurythmics, Bronski Beat* & *The Communards* as Annie Lennox and Jimmy Somerville are both Scottish, and don't forget Mark Knopfler was born and raised in Glasgow (until he was seven) so we can add *Dire McStraits* too - oh and *Spandau Ballet* wore kilts once. So it's pretty easy to argue that all the best pop music of the 1980s was actually Scottish.

Now you might think that I'm starting to push my luck a bit here, however I feel I need to point out that back in those days the threshold for proof of Scottishness was set considerably higher than it is today. In recent years, the bar has been lowered to the point where anyone who has even thought about having a roll & square sausage is likely to be given serious consideration for citizenship.

But with a relatively small population, you can kind of understand our willingness to throw the warm tartan shawl of inclusion over a slightly wider community (if only to give us more of a fighting chance in the Six Nations Rugby Championships).

Ok, so we've not quite got to the stage of pulling people in off the street, however we have managed to convince ourselves that JK Rowling is Scottish purely based on the fact that she decided to pop into a coffee shop in Edinburgh while she was writing a book.

But back in the 80s, the qualification criteria were much more rigorous and so to have so many genuine Scottish artists topping the charts was really quite something. We definitely punched above our weight in all divisions of the music scene.

Even the legendary Abbey Road Studios were positively fizzing with Irn Bru as the serenading Scottish songsters strutted their stuff. And it's highly likely that many of the artists who weren't Scottish probably wished they had been as that's where all the action was.

In fact with a little bit of imagination (even if it's just an illusion) you can create your own 1980s 'Glasgow' bands like:

- *Frankie Goes to Williamwood*
- *The Easterhouse Martins*
- *Orchestral Manoeuvres in Queens Park*
- *Belinda Carmyle*
- *CeCe Dennistoun*
- *Bruce Springburn*
- *Whitney Bellahouston*
- *Rouken Glenn Medeiros*
- *KD Langside*
- *Ruchazie Fantayzee*
- *Ibroxy Music*
- *Spandau Swally*
- *Buckfast Fizz*

While you're making your mind up about that lot, let's leave the land of make believe and get back to reality...

As if the exceptional eighties music wasn't enough, we also had a fusion of fabulously flashy fashion to *squeeze* ourselves into.

1980s pop style was bold & brash, with garish luminous colours, stonewashed jeans and extremely embarrassing leg warmers. We also had Madonna inspired fingerless gloves and some tremendous hats (thanks to Boy George). However unfortunately we also saw stirrup pants, leather trench coats and way too much athletic-inspired streetwear. We also got into some terrible habits like tucking our tasteless jumpers into our distressed denims and rolling up the sleeves of our oversized jackets. We have *Miami Vice* to blame for that one. Thanks for nothing Don Johnson (even if your granny was probably Scottish).

Although we had *Spandex* in the eighties, we didn't actually have *Spanx* so you just had to hold yourself in by developing advanced muscle control from attending sweaty aerobics classes in athletic-inspired streetwear. It certainly seemed to work for *The Kids from Fame*. (Hang on - I've just realised that we had footless tights as well as fingerless gloves. What on earth was all that about? Why were we so determined to expose our extremities? It all seemed very [Steve] strange).

Which brings me on to the curious craze of men applying cosmetics to their *visages*. 1970s Glam Rock had given the ok to guys wearing eyeshadow, but the New Romantic devotees took this to a whole new level (42).

We witnessed men's *coupons** become almost unrecognisable under layers of impeccably applied slap. And this was only 'topped' by the amount of hairspray needed to keep their massive 'dos in place.

I could never quite get my hair to look like the guys in *ABC* but I did love their look in The Look of Love. (Although ABC weren't actually Scottish, their lead singer was called Martin Fry which makes him sound Scottish as we fry pretty much everything).

So it was big hair, big makeup, big blouses and big shoulder pads (and it was much the same for the women). In fact for the first time, straight couples were able to share their entire wardrobes (presuming of course they were roughly the same size).

[**coupon**: face]

My mum was never very comfortable with me wearing makeup but I was *adam-ant* that I wanted to give it a go. She said I had perfect skin so why would I want to cover it up? To be honest, I couldn't really see what all the *commotion* was about.

But let's talk about men's hair in the 80s and celebrate some of the more memorable masters of the mullet. There were that many coiffured contenders that narrowing them down became a case of 'perm' any two from five. The top slots were taken by Paul King (of *King*) and the not at all too shy Limahl from *Kajagoogoo*. The judges had to 'comb-over' hours of footage to select the winner and had great difficulty 'parting' these two legends of the locks. They were a 'cut' above the rest with Limahl being the obvious 'highlight'. (There was definitely some mousse loose aboot his hoose). However the undisputed winner of '*Biggest Male Hair of the Decade*' had to be the lovable Love & Pride frontman as he was the only one to do it without the aid of a *Van de Graaff generator*.

But it was a gravelly Welsh singer who would blow (dry) us away with her breathtaking bouffant. Bonnie Tyler's massive shaggy do was nearly visible from space which was quite ironic as she was partly responsible for the hole in the ozone layer due to the amount of hairspray she skooshed over her napper. I just wish I'd had the foresight to invest in L'Oreal *Elnett* shares in the 1980s as you could barely breathe for the stuff.

I went to a 1980s reunion recently and due to my receding hairline I ended up popping into a fancy dress shop to buy a wig. They had very nearly sold out however fortunately I managed to get the *Last of the Mohicans*.

Anyway back to the music. The 1980s served us up a smörgåsbord of jazz-funk, synth-pop, new wave and hip-hop. We were boogieing away in our big blouses to the slappy bass of Mark King of Level 42 and the synthy-dancey vibes of *Depeche Mode* and the *Pet Shop Boys*.

But sadly, not every item on this modern-day music menu was to everyone's taste. We'd started to see a bit of lyrical censorship in the seventies with the Sex Pistols, however it was the eighties that really got the goat of the grammatical gestapo. Frankie said RELAX but the BBC wouldn't. Their banning of the song turned it into one of the biggest selling singles in UK pop history.

Holly and the guys clearly spotted that they were on to a winner as their next single 'Two Tribes' also topped the charts the following summer after the video got banned due to cold war paranoia. You just can't beat a good ban!

George Michael then managed to get in on the act with 'I Want Your Sex' and Madonna raised some well-manicured eyebrows with 'Like a Virgin' and 'Like a Prayer'. In fact Madge was churning them out like a good 'un!

The mad world of song suppression got a little bit madder when MTV banned the video for *Queen*'s synth-pop classic 'I Want to Break Free' presumably because they didn't like watching men doing the hoovering. It was all a bit ironic as MTV went on to become one of the biggest supporters of the LGBTQ+ community, so why on planet earth would they ban a camped-up Coronation Street piss take? I mean for the love of the common people, were the MTV bosses just being obtuse? I'm not sure what their angle was (other than it being between 90 and 180 degrees).

However there's one bit of 80s pop censorship which still shocks me to this day. How the fuck did Olivia Newton-John get on the list? I mean the *Grease* goddess was the very essence of sweet and innocent, goody two shoes, girl-next-door-ness. In fact she was so squeaky clean that she even had the pish ripped out of her by the pink ladies.

Let's get Physical? Let's get sensible more like. Ok so we did get a brief glimpse of her in the shower at one point and there was a little bit of a homoerotic theme towards the end when two very handsome, oil-skinned, muscular men in *Speedos* held hands. But come on? When someone like lovely Liv gets a music video veto then the rest of us might as well pack up and go home.

One of the other slightly bizarre episodes in the mid 80s was when three different artists all came up with the same ingenious plan for a unique song title: 'The Power of Love'. A superb idea that nobody else could possibly have thought of. Really?

Remarkably all three versions of the song got released within a nine-month period from December 1984 to August 1985, with Jennifer Rush sandwiched between Holly Johnson & Huey Lewis. (Now, now - that's how rumours start...)

Amazingly, they all made it to number one in the charts (Huey in the US and the other two in the UK), and it gave *Frankie Goes to Hollywood* their third consecutive chart topper in just over 12 months.

The Frankies had thrown down the gauntlet to the rest of the music world and then slapped them right in the coupon with it. Talk about the power of glove...

LIVE AID

The 1980s were almost perfectly bisected by one of the most audacious concerts in music history.

On 13th July 1985, *LIVE AID* brought together a dazzling array of global artists under two roofs. (Well, no roofs actually as both venues were open air but you get what I mean). It was also the setting for one of *Queen*'s greatest live performances. They only played for twenty-two minutes but it still got voted as the greatest rock gig of all time by a poll of music industry experts in 2005.

Freddie had the audience eating out of his hand with his now iconic call-and-response "*ay-oh*" singalong. His final sustained "*aaaaaaay-oh*" became known as 'the note heard around the world'.

His doctor had advised him not to perform at LIVE AID due to the 'poor boy' having a vocal strain. We're all eternally grateful that Freddie didn't give a shit about what his doctor thought.

There were a few other side stories to the day like when Sir Elton John welcomed George Michael on stage to sing 'Don't Let the Sun Go Down on Me'. He nearly forgot to introduce Andrew Ridgely who had also turned up on stage to perform as a backing singer. Oops!

There was also a very public fall out between Led Zeppelin and Phil Collins. A couple of months before the gig, Phil had asked Robert Plant if he could accompany them on the night and Plant had agreed. However, they'd clearly forgotten all about it until Phil turned up on stage. Jimmy Page slated Collins for not knowing any of the songs and Phil felt he had been unfairly scapegoated for what was an unrehearsed, poorly performed and pretty dreadful

Led Zep reunion gig. The performance was plagued by technical issues meaning that nobody could really hear each other and so it ended up being a bit of a disaster. The former Genesis frontman probably felt a bit pissed off after going to all the effort of jumping on *Concorde* so that he could be the only artist to play on both sides of the Atlantic. He probably wished he'd left his sticks in the overhead locker. In fact during the set I suspect he was looking for one of the overwing exits (which should have been clearly marked and illuminated by floor level lighting).

But despite the distinctly iffy performance on the night, Phil's supersonic gesture to appear at both venues was still seen as a '*cymbal*' of unity between the UK and USA. (Ba-dum tish!)

However one of the biggest LIVE AID stories was about an 18-year old high school student from sunny Florida. Bernard Watson camped out for a week before the US event and eventually managed to convince the Philadelphia concert producer to let him open the show. Which he did. What a hero.

The full line up was:

LONDON/WEMBLEY

Status Quo, The Style Council, The Boomtown Rats, Adam Ant, Ultravox, Spandau Ballet, Elvis Costello, Nik Kershaw, Sade, Sting & Phil Collins, Howard Jones, Bryan Ferry, Paul Young & Alison Moyet, U2, Dire Straits, Queen, David Bowie, The Who, Elton John & George Michael, Paul McCartney, and the star-studded cast of *Band Aid* with 'Do They Know it's Christmas'.

PHILADELPHIA/JFK

Bernard Watson, Joan Baez, The Hooters, The Four Tops, Billy Ocean, Black Sabbath, Run-DMC, Rick Springfield, REO Speedwagon, Crosby Stills & Nash, Judas Priest, Bryan Adams, The Beach Boys, George Thorogood, Simple Minds, The Pretenders, Santana, Ashford & Simpson, Madonna, Tom Petty, Kenny Loggins, The Cars, Neil Young, The Power Station, The Thomson Twins, Eric Clapton, Phil Collins, Led Zeppelin, Crosby Stills Nash & Young, Duran Duran, Patti Labelle, Hall & Oates, Mick Jagger & Tina Turner, Bob Dylan (with *Ronnie Wood* & *Keith Richards*), and finally the star-spangled banner waving, sunglass-wearing, pearly-white toothed cast of *USA for Africa* singing 'We Are the World'.

***

As we started to ease ourselves into the 1990s, the music got a bit more diverse and I remember hearing a song on the radio that I really liked and went into my local HMV to buy the CD. The only problem was that I didn't know the name of the song or the artist. However I was confident that my humming ability would see me through. So I said to the guy "Have you got that new CD with the song that goes: *Ey-ay, hay-ya, oh-ay, hay-ya. Ey-ay, hay-ya, oh-ay, hay-ya-ya"*.

He said, "Absolutely big man - I know exactly the one you mean" and stuck it in one of those small square bespoke CD bags with a seal around the top to show you'd actually paid for it. I left the shop happy and excited to get it spinning on my new *JVC UX-1 micro system* (with *active hyper bass*). Needless to say it bore absolutely no resemblance to the song I wanted.

So I wandered into another store the next day and chatted to an even more confident record shop assistant who assured me 100% that he knew the one I was after. He didn't...

Seven CD purchases later (yes, 7), I finally got myself a copy of *'Cross of Changes'* by German new-age project *Enigma* which (thank God) included the hypnotic chanting masterpiece *'Return to Innocence'*. I felt like going back to all the other record shops and saying *"Ey-ay, hay - ya BASTARD!"*

It's interesting to note that the chant in the track is actually a traditional Amis drinking song from Taiwan sung by folk duo *Difang* & *Igay Duana*. However it transpired that the recording was used without their permission resulting in the happy couple receiving all of the royalties. Well done *Difang* and *Igay* and the Taiwanese music community. I'm delighted to have contributed in some small way to supporting your efforts.

Which reminds me of the story of the Scottish guy who bought a pair of shoes and when he opened the box there was one slip-on and one lace up. He turned over the shoes and the label said "Taiwan"...

CLATT PATS

CHAPTER TWO

CLATTY PATS

Its official name was Cleopatra's Nightclub however nobody ever called it that. Clatty Pats was a Glasgow institution. Its most notable feature was that it had really sticky carpets. In fact the floor was stickier than a sticky bun covered in sticky toffee pudding. Everyone talked about it and it became the reason most people wanted to go there just so they could say they had experienced it.

They should really have lifted that carpet. In fact they could have done that fairly easily by just 'sticking' on a Michael Jackson number and asking everyone to moonwalk in the same direction.

There was also a stuffed camel at one end of the dancefloor (yes, honestly) and the popularity of Clatty's was intrinsically linked to these two almost surreal aspects of the venue. However, it also served fairly inexpensive booze and there weren't many other clubbing options in Glasgow's west end, and so it continued to be where many of us went for our teenage kicks until the early 2000s.

I always thought it was quite fitting that the combination of a camel and a sticky floor meant that people would often walk like an Egyptian without actually realising it. However after a skinful of the cheap stuff, they would inevitably end up walking like a Glaswegian.

There was a bar underneath which at the end of the eighties became *L'Académie* - a pseudo French boozérie with faux leather chesterfield sofas and modestly priced pretentious cocktails. However, it was very much the lesser known of the two venues as its upstairs neighbour was nothing short of a national legend.

I remember one of my sister-in-law's brothers (who had taken responsibility for organising that year's family Christmas do) proudly announcing that he'd found this amazing little French restaurant that was doing an incredible deal on festive lunches. It was only £8.95 for a three course dinner (including dancing). It sounded too good to be true and most definitely was.

For some inexplicable reason our table for 14 was positioned right in the middle of the dance floor which was surrounded on all sides by cosy couches. So we were sat directly in the gaze of disgruntled punters with folded arms and menacing stares who looked thoroughly pissed off that we were hogging half of the available dancing space.

Things didn't improve when the grub arrived. We were served up what can only be described as lukewarm unseasoned soup followed by *Bernard Matthews* thinly sliced turkey breast (which wasn't bootiful), rubber roast potatoes and anaemic veg. The dessert was a barely heated *Mr Kipling* mince pie with the silver foil case marks still visible. Charging £8.95 for this was one of the most shocking crimes Glasgow had ever witnessed (...and that's saying something).

At one point I nipped off to the gents and met the DJ who was standing at the neighbouring stall. I asked him how it was going and he replied: "Aye fine big man - apart from the bunch of fannies having their Christmas dinner in the middle of the fucking dance floor."

The city centre provided a much broader selection of trendy nightspots like Maestros, The Cotton Club, Ultratheque, The Savoy, Bennetts, Charlie Parkers and the legendary Victoria's, where you could cut the atmosphere with a knife (and occasionally some of the punters too). It brought a whole new meaning to the term 'going for a slash'...

Glasgow had transformed itself into much more of a funkytown in the mid-80s and one of the trendiest spots was Custom House Quay on the Clyde. It was home to Waves & Spankies which later became Manhattan and then Panama Jax.

A few years later, Henry Afrikas moved to the same waterfront location from its previous home in York Street. Sadly, I rarely managed to gain entry into any of these trendier establishments. I obviously just had one of those faces (...or it might have been the legwarmers).

At the end of the eighties Glasgow got its very own floating nightclub - the *Tuxedo Princess*. The Boogie Boat became an instant favourite amongst the local clubbing contingent and it even had a revolving dancefloor (...or maybe it just felt that way after a few Campari & sodas).

There was always the chance of spotting your favourite footballing star of the day as they seemed to spend much more of their time on the water than on the training ground. The Tux was a firm favourite and as it turned out, an Old Firm favourite too. You would often find local legends like Ally McCoist and 'Champagne' Charlie Nicholas holding court somewhere on board.

One of the other footy frequenters at the time was Mo Johnston, the blonde bombshell who will forever be remembered as the man who crossed the religious divide. However, he wasn't the first post war Catholic to play for Rangers. That title rests with Alfie Conn, however 'Super Mo' was the only one to do it in the 80s. But he nearly wasn't the only one...

Frank *'where's the burdz'* McAvennie had been propositioned three years earlier by the then Rangers boss Graeme Souness. But he turned him down on the basis that he was too much of a Celtic fan. It was almost certainly the only time Macca has ever turned down any sort of proposition. Frisky Frank was a regular fixture on the Love Boat and apparently his scoring record was pretty impressive. He achieved all this success despite having a hairdo like a bag of monster munch. Mind you, his teeth were fabulous. Some guys have all the luck.

In its early days the Princess was pretty posh and you even had to wear a tie to get in on a Saturday night. There was a chic restaurant called *Di Angelos* as well as several cocktail bars and a piano lounge. However its status as a stylish nightspot started to veer off course in the 90s and it became much more of a rave venue before sailing off down the coast back to Newcastle to see out its final days on the Tyne.

If you wanted slightly more excitement than a boaty boogie and a Bacardi, then Glasgow's *Grand Ole Opry* might just have been the place for you...

It was a somewhat unlikely musical mecca based on the south side of the river. It had a saloon bar, bingo hall and a massive stage where country & western bands would perform every weekend to a delighted horde of highly accomplished line dancers. They even had live gun-slinging demonstrations re-enacted by Stetson wearing cowboys with huge belts and bootlace ties (who I presume lived locally). The gunfights were a surreal and slightly scary highlight of a magnificent night of yankee *yee-ha*.

Obviously they were firing blanks (like many men my age). Some of the 'chaps' even wore spurs & holsters, which was a little bit disconcerting as you were queueing up at the chuck wagon for a hot dog. However things got back to a semblance of normality during the post shoot-out raffle (all proceeds to charity of course).

This legendary venue is still open today. Y'all should go along sometime and say howdy! (Sorry, got a wee bit carried away there...)

The majority of my clubbing time was spent at the *Extension Disco* at Glasgow University Union (now called the HIVE). Jim, the resident DJ used to serve us up a delicious assortment of bangers at his self-styled *'Friday Night Music Delight'* & *'Saturday Sound Sensation'*, where you could dance yourself dizzy to the latest in jazz-funk & hip-hop. It had a cocktail bar upstairs where you could continue to get to know your dancefloor dalliances in relative peace & quiet.

The Extension disco was often a very popular warm-up spot before you headed over to Clatty's to finish off your night in complete chaos.

SPECIAL BREW?

It was a stroke of genius. Call your pub something that doesn't really sound like a pub and it will be permanently rammed with people pretending to their other halves that they're just popping out for a coffee and an amaretti biscuit. However, staggering through your front door six hours later reeking of *'au de Tennent's'* took a bit of explaining. The *Queen's Park Café* still makes me chuckle when I drive down Victoria Road.

Although I grew up fairly close to Queens Park, the majority of my (legal age) drinking was done in the west end as I had started at Glasgow Uni when I was 18½. The variety of bars on the west side of the city was vast and funnily enough there was even one called the *Variety Bar* (not too far from the *Canton Express* which you'll hear about later).

Uisge Beatha was one of my favourite pubs in the late eighties. It was bloody huge with several adjoining rooms that you had to traipse up and down several times to find your friends. But it was well worth the effort as it was always packed and the atmosphere was magic. It occupied a handy spot on Woodlands Road which was a convenient halfway house on your way back into town.

Tennent's Bar has a location to die for on the corner of Byres Road & Highburgh Road and so consequently swallowed up a large proportion of the west end drinking population. It remains an absolute banker for big footy matches and has an impressive selection of cask ales. You can also get a tasty cheap lunch and it's now got a comedy club downstairs which one of my pal's pals performed at recently.

Curlers Rest has been around since Roman times and is positioned right next door to your public transport home (if you're going underground). It was home to the Partick Curling Club in the 1800s and apparently King Charles II visited in the late 1600s but had to wake up the landlord to get a pint. Hopefully the current King Chic will get the chance to pop in at some point and enjoy a slightly improved level of customer service.

Curlers can legitimately claim to be one of the oldest pubs in Scotland - although pretty much every old-ish pub will try and make that assertion. To be fair, the records were a bit flaky back then so it's hard to check. The *Scotia Bar* and the *'Sarry Heid'* are also fairly prehistoric, and even our local pub in Drymen claims to be the oldest licensed premises in Scotland which I'm sure it probably is (maybe).

Bonhams in Byres Road was the first proper wine bar in the west end (ooohh check us out!). A great place to take a prospective girlfriend/boyfriend if you wanted to pretend you were much posher than you actually were. It became a popular hangout for west end girls.

The *Beer Bar* at Glasgow University Union (the GUU) provided exactly what it said on the tin. The selection of brews on offer was tremendous and you could get a pie and beans (and a pint) for virtually nothing. It always seemed to be full of familiar faces and had a lovely earthy, pubby smell to it. It also had a *'dunny'* (basement) which was the perfect spot for a game of darts or a sing song.

[Full disclosure]: I was probably in the Beer Bar every day when I was a student (and quite a lot of days when I wasn't). So it will always be the kind of place I feel I never can say goodbye to. Which is probably why I've devoted an entire chapter to the GUU later in the book.

The Baby Grand was another Glasgow stalwart which finally closed its piano lid in 2025. It had opened in 1984 and another one of my pals became a part owner during the 90s. The food was always excellent and I remember popping in there after Scotland won the Five Nations Grand Slam in 1990 (although I'm not sure I can remember leaving).

Forty years is a pretty impressive shift for any pub under the same ownership. I played the grand piano there on a few occasions however I feel I should point out that they never actually asked me to.

Within a stone's throw of *The Baby Grand* (if you're a good stone thrower) is *The Griffin* on Bath Street. It was dangerously close to where I worked in the late 80s and you could get a pub lunch (including a pint) for only £1.50. With prices like that, it's not surprising that the lunches could be quite long (often lasting several weeks). The service was exceptional and it ran like a well-oiled machine, which probably explains why the clientele ended up in a similar state.

The Rock Garden in Queen Street probably deserves to have a whole book devoted to it based on the pivotal role it played as a cultural mecca for the Scottish pop music community in the 1980s.

The Clash famously played in the basement of the Rock in 1985 which further cemented the venue's near iconic status, and *Hipsway* was 'hewn from the Rock' after a fortuitous chat between the barman and the former bass player from *Altered Images*.

***

I'm very conscious that I might not have mentioned your favourite 1980s west end Glasgow pub. There are of course plenty of others that I remember like the Aragon, the Rubaiyat, the Doublet, the Dolphin, the Bothy, the Arlington, The Ben Nevis, The Park Bar, The Islay Inn, The Three Judges, Wilson's and the Wickets Hotel in Partick. However I didn't spend quite as much time in those so the memories are a bit more sketchy.

Oh - and I didn't spend *all* my time in pubs...

Tinseltown
in the Sun
IRN BRU

CHAPTER THREE

TINSELTOWN IN THE SUN

They say that Scottish weather is a bit unpredictable. That's not strictly true. There are really only ever two possibilities: Pure roastin' and pure baltic.

Billy Connolly famously said: *"There's no such thing as bad weather, just the wrong clothing"*. A very profound and insightful statement, although he even more famously danced around Picadilly Circus with no clothing (or 'in the scud' as we say around these parts).

Glaswegians don't seem to have the ability to regulate their own body temperatures (a bit like dogs

I suppose). However at least dogs can pant in public without getting arrested.

Many Glasgow inhabitants will save up all year to go on a fortnight's holiday to Spain and then come back after three days because it's too hot. Our skin isn't really designed for heat and we're fairly easy to spot on a crowded beach. Which reminds me of the story of the Glasgow woman who went into M&S to buy herself a 'skin tone' vest. She was very upset when the assistant handed her a white one (as she actually wanted blue).

Anyway at least she was planning to wear one unlike the majority of the male Glasgow population when there's even a hint of sunshine.

I remember once speaking to a guy who had one of those Porsche 911s which had a rear spoiler which apparently raised automatically at 50mph and came back down at 3mph.

The *'Taps aff'* tradition operates on much the same principle. They automatically come *'aff'* at 12°C and then go back on in November.

During the summer months, Glasgow city centre is positively hoaching with hordes of topless men. In fact if you're a guy under forty and have your tap *'oan'*, you'll probably look very out of place (unless you're in Park Circus).

Scotland's biggest city centre also has a proud tradition of pop-up retail outlets. Argyle Street has been home to many of the world's biggest brands, but it has also been a platform for some of the more enterprising 'niche' offerings:

Erra Sports Socks - two furra poun'

When I first heard this attractive proposition, I'd presumed that all the merchandise was Irish (i.e. Éire Sports Socks, Éire Gas Lighters, Éire Xmas Paper etc.) Our Glasgow street traders are a very resourceful bunch and are capable of exploiting new trends at the drop of a festive hat.

We shouldn't really be surprised about this as Scotland has a very proud history of innovation and has traditionally led the world in new discoveries. In fact I think it's fair to say that the Scots invented pretty much everything that's of any use.

Here's just a few of the more notable ones:

- The Telephone
- The Television
- The Fax Machine
- RADAR
- The Steam Engine
- The Bicycle
- The Toaster
- The Lawnmower
- Tarmac
- Penicillin
- Chloroform
- The Fridge
- The Raincoat (obviously)
- The Flushing Toilet
- Modern Economics
- Golf
- Haggis
- Grand Theft Auto
- Dolly the sheep
- Irn Bru
- Chicken Tikka Masala

I rest my case. Anyway, back to the shopping…

Glasgow has always offered a diverse mix of retail therapy and the eighties saw the beginning of the transition from the traditional big department stores (which Glasgow had loads of) to some slightly more trendy and fashionable boutiques like *Cruise* on Renfield Street and *The Warehouse* on the corner of Glassford Street and Wilson Street.

However the biggest shift was the arrival of American style shopping malls like *Princess Square* which opened in 1986 and the *St Enoch Centre* three years later. Although a handful of the traditional department stores survived, sadly most of them are now just a distant memory. *Lewis's* on Argyle Street became *Debenhams* at the start of the 90s and lasted pretty well until COVID did for it in 2021.

Frasers was bought by *Sports Direct* which still seems about the weirdest thing I've ever heard. The others I remember from the 80s were:

Forsyths

Posh togs and school uniforms that Brucie would've been proud of (if he played his cards right).

Arnott's

Similar to *Lewis's/Debenhams*. Closed its doors in 1994 to a chorus of *"We Arnott impressed!"*

Watt Brothers

Great for quality household items. Perfect as a one-stop-shop for all your Christmas presents. Closed in 2019 to a chorus of *"Watt the f*ck?"*

Trerons

A kind of Scottish *Harrods* offering high end luxury & elegance. Burned to the ground in 1986 to a chorus of *"Can you smell something?"*

BHS, Littlewoods* and *C&A

All known for their affordable clothing and cheapish in-store restaurants. It's a sin that all three of these retail titans are now closed for good.

Goldbergs

Closed in 1990 and was bought by the Weisfeld's who owned *What Every Woman Wants* (which was a kind of 1980s *TK Maxx*). However that too ended up closing in 2003 as it turned out that it wasn't what every woman wanted.

Chelsea Girl

A real fashion hub which became *River Island* at the end of the 1980s. The 'island' is still around today however it's now surrounded by troubled waters as the river 'bank' is running short of dosh.

Oh, and who could forget that ***John Menzies*** had a cylindrical store in central station. Well done John!

***

Glasgow's popularity got a significant boost in the 80s with the *GLASGOW'S MILES BETTER* campaign which culminated in the *Glasgow Garden Festival* taking place in 1988. A couple of years later, Glasgow graced the international stage with our year in the spotlight as *European Capital of Culture.*

Glasgow had celebrated its 800th anniversary in the mid-70s and that became the springboard for a massive charm offensive for Scotland's biggest city.

The *Glasgow's Miles Better* strapline (with a smiling *Mr Happy* from the *Mister Men* as the 'O') is still widely regarded as one of the most successful urban rebranding exercises ever undertaken.

The bit I loved most was when the PR team suggested targeting tourists who were attending the Edinburgh Festival that year by sticking ads on the side of Edinburgh buses. The capital city's council took great umbrage at the suggestion and decided to ban the campaign. Within a few days the story of Edinburgh banning Glasgow had gone 'viral' and even made the front page of the Wall Street Journal. It turned out to be the best piece of global publicity that Glasgow could ever have wished for. Thank you Edinburgh. May there always be sunshine on Leith!

Don't forget that Glasgow had previously suffered from a reputation of being a hard-drinking, violent, gang-ridden city and so the slogan which morphed into *Glasgow 'Smiles' Better* tapped into the idea that Glasgow was much the friendlier of the two rivals and that we would never want to take ourselves too seriously.

The 1988 *Glasgow Garden Festival* ran from mid-April until the end of September which was perfect timing for me as I had just finished Uni. The maths had worked out very well too as it was exactly fifty years since the *Glasgow Empire Exhibition* of 1938 and was the centenary of the *International Exhibition of Science, Art & Industry*. So Glasgow ended up being a shoo-in for the garden festival gig.

The location on the south bank of the Clyde was perfect and the main attractions were a fabulous riverside rollercoaster, a 240 foot revolving viewing tower, a Mississippi style paddle steamer, a quirky miniature railway and an assortment of extremely wacky giant props including a fork, a trowel and a garden tap. There was also a brand new swivelling swing bridge (ooohh check us out!) which connected the festival site to what was the Scottish Exhibition Centre (SEC), now the SECC.

There was also a bit of a musical element to the festival with a fairly wide-ranging selection of live performances every day. They even had an on-site recording studio where you could get your own stuff on tape. Our band at the time (*The Folkal Chords*) performed there resulting in the unexpected bonus of us all getting a free pass for the whole of the festival (including unlimited goes on the *Coca-Cola* rollercoaster). Now that was definitely a perk well worth having!

During its five month stint, it attracted more than four million visitors and was by far the most successful of the five national UK Garden Festivals. One of the *Taggart* episodes was filmed on location at the festival site and it's now home to the *Glasgow Science Centre* and is also the main media campus for *BBC Scotland* and *STV.*

Glasgow's decade in the spotlight ended with our year as *European Capital of Culture* in 1990 with the most notable events being a Van Gogh exhibition at the Burrell Collection and a gigantic free music festival held across four city centre venues. The mega gig featured bands like: *Texas, Big Country, Wet Wet Wet, Hue & Cry* and *Deacon Blue.* There were also live performances from *The Hothouse Flowers, The Average White Band, Love and Money, The Silencers, Eddi Reader, John Martyn* and *Billy Bragg* (who sang with Natalie Merchant & Michael Stipe from *REM*).

More than 250,000 people attended *'The Big Day'* on 3rd of June and the only regrettable incident was when Sheena Easton got pelted with missiles by buckfasted bams for sounding a bit too American. However, fortunately the only thing she got hit with was a glowstick which was much less damaging than an empty bottle of vitamin 'B'. Thank buck for that.

We also had live concerts from *Frank Sinatra, Pavarotti* and the *Rolling Stones.* Weren't we gemmy!

***

It feels quite fitting that I started writing this book in the year Glasgow celebrated its 850th anniversary. I quite like round numbers...

STRICTLY FUN
DANCING

CHAPTER FOUR

STRICTLY FUN DANCING

Ceilidhs are brilliant. Ceilidh dancing is by far the most enjoyable thing you can do in a kilt and it's unusual in the fact that the worse you are at it the more enjoyable it is.

However, I have a friend who hates ceilidhs. Now just to be clear, I'm a firm believer in embracing other people's perspectives and taking on different points of view. But he's wrong. He's completely & utterly wrong.

A well synchronised *Strip the Willow* is a thing of beauty, especially the bit at the end when both sides of the line are flying around in sync. Even the slightly more sedate *Gay Gordons* is a very difficult thing not to tap your feet to. The steps are actually pretty straightforward and it only takes you a few ceilidhs to get your 'C' legs, after which you just can't get enough!

Some ceilidh bands have dance instructors (or 'callers') to help out the first timers. However I think this is a terrible idea. It would be much better if the band just said:

> *"Aw stuff it - just birl round with your partner and have a right good laugh".*

Ceilidh dancing is one of the few activities Scottish people can do which can help them live longer (that's presuming of course you don't actually die during the performance). One place you could ceilidh with unrestrained joy and freedom was *The Riverside Club* on Fox Street near the Clyde. You would have to queue for hours to then pack in like sardines, which kind of defeated the purpose a bit as it was almost impossible to find enough space to dance. However it only seemed to add to the overall experience and the queueing start time gradually wound back from around half six on a Friday or Saturday to something like 4 o'clock the previous Tuesday.

To be fair, it was a much safer pursuit than most Glasgow weekend activities. There was never any trouble at a ceilidh and the only real risk was being struck by the flying limbs of an uncoordinated beginner. It was great fun and gave you a seriously good workout too. I'm sure many went along to the *Riverside Club* hoping to meet their own 'Dashing White Sergeant'. However if they did, he would probably have been sweatier than Prince Andrew on his way back from Pizza Hut.

I remember one night we were there, a group of seemingly random people suddenly brought the place to life with some exquisitely synchronised Irish step dancing. Coincidentally they were called *The McLaughlins* and they were bloody brilliant.

This was long before Michael Flatley had been invented and their choreography was tighter than Olivia Newton-John's *Grease* trousers. At first it just seemed like a few pals wanting to show off a bit, but gradually more and more people joined in and then came together in an immaculately formed line for the big finale. It was superb! I suppose it was a bit like an early version of a *'flash mob'* (although they hadn't been invented either).

Sadly the club is no longer around but you can still hear the accordions and the heuchs! *

WEST END BIRLS

Another cracking 80s ceilidh venue was *The Park Bar* near Kelvingrove. The pub equivalent of Glasgow's Gaelic capital. You can almost feel the breeze of the Hebrides and many highlanders & islanders feel an irresistible urge to camp out there for weeks. It's not hard to see why as the live music is fabulous and we had many memorable nights there while we were students. Their selection of single malts is fantastic however the dancefloor is pretty small which might explain why it's often described as a place where you're guaranteed to bump into old friends.

[**heuch**: expressing exhilaration or delight, particularly while dancing to a reel or jig]

There were a sizeable number of people who moved to Glasgow from Barra and South Uist in the 1960s and *The Park Bar* played an important role in bringing that community together.

It was also 'instrumental' in keeping Gaelic alive in the central belt. I can clearly remember the *Cùm Gàidhlig Beò* campaign getting into full swing in the mid-eighties (particularly the car stickers).

The *Glasgow Gaelic School* opened in 1985 and I'm sure it's no accident that it was a five minute walk from *The Park Bar* (not that I'm suggesting for a moment that any of the teaching staff enjoyed a wee dram occasionally). It's now more than 130 years old and is still absolutely jumping almost every night (and most Sunday afternoons too).

One of the great things about ceilidh dancing is that you have a bit of scope to do some freestyling and even introduce some of your own choreography.

The *Eightsome Reel* even has a kind of 'guest slot' built into the routine so that each of the eight participants gets the chance for a solo. Pretty much anything goes (well, almost anything…)

At our wedding ceilidh, one of my pals (who's also my dentist) did the *'Walk Like an Egyptian'* moves during his spotlight jig (despite the fact he's actually Italian). It was absolutely hilarious and I was literally dancing with tears in my eyes.

We'd selected our wedding reception venue purely based on the size of the dancefloor. It was absolutely colossal but was still completely rammed for the whole night.

I also had a ceilidh at my twenty-first birthday party and I had pre-rehearsed a backflip which I performed (in a kilt) during one of the group dances. I think in gymnastics they call it a 'back handspring' but whatever it's called it wasn't an official part of the routine and Craig Revel Horwood would have been raging. I still have photographic evidence of this ill-judged manoeuvre and my camera never lies. However it's a bit blurry so I'm not sure whether anyone actually saw the whole of the moon. I guess it was my take on a Scottish version of 'Flashdance'. ...what a feeling!

All of this just goes to show that ceilidhs are good for the soul and you can't beat jigging around in random directions to Scottish dance music. In fact you could say that it's a kind of magic…

***

Now I know we're all thinking it, so it would be very remiss of me not to mention Scotland's other national dance. *The Slosh…*

It has long been a staple of weddings and birthday parties and even the slightest hint that Daniel Boone might be on the DJ's playlist will guarantee you an impeccable performance of the iconic Lanarkshire line dance. In fact any Glaswegian over the age of fifty will be able to give you a flawless demonstration (even if you don't really want them to).

Sunday morning, up with the lark
Think I'll take a walk in the park
Hey, hey, hey, it's a beautiful day…

Other dance styles are available, but nothing beats going for a *Slosh…*

Barra

CHAPTER FIVE

BARRA

A rite of passage for many Glaswegians was to go somewhere even colder, wetter and windier for your holidays. The Outer Hebrides ticked all these boxes.

One of my friends had a tenuous highland connection which resulted in us getting free use of an empty schoolhouse at the remote north end of Barra for a week during the summer break. Eoligarry is one of those stunning Scottish locations where on a warm sunny day it looks more Caribbean than Hebridean.

But unfortunately that only happens once every five years and this wasn't one of them.

The accommodation arrangement was a kind of weather-proof camping affair where we just had our sleeping bags spread out on the gym hall floor. Perfectly comfortable when you're in your late teens and verging on what we would now call glamping (minus the mud and exorbitant pricing).

We were on a limited budget and had been given permission to access the school canteen larder and help ourselves (within reason) to any items still in date which hadn't already been snaffled by hungry Hebridean weans. The most valuable find was a tin of 50 *Westlers jumbo sized hot dog sausages.* We weren't quite sure whether these were included in the 'within reason' category, however needs must and all that…

The scenery at the north tip of Barra is both rugged and beautiful. I had my guitar with me and we would head down to the pristine white sandy beach at night and sing songs round a driftwoody fire. It was as good as life got. We would wake every morning to another day in paradise and then attempt to hitch a lift to Castlebay, the vibrant(ish) capital of the island and the location of the main pub.

During our stay, we discovered that the Barra *Fèis* (festival) was on which meant there was slightly more happening than normal. One of the highlights was the *'Barra Olympics'*, and fortunately I'd brought some suitably sporty clothing and footwear.

There was a mix of both highland & lowland events and our mob did pretty well considering we'd done zero training and it was blowing a hoolie. Two of us ended up making the podium in the high jump, the men's 800m and the pillow fight, which felt like a fairly respectable result in the circumstances. There were no medals unfortunately, just warm cans of *Tennent's* and inaudible applause (due to the wind).

It had only been a year or two since we'd competed at school athletics events so that probably stood us in fairly good stead. However not all of our previous results were an entirely accurate reflection of the performances. Let me explain...

My mum was a maths teacher at our school and despite her not being an official member of the PE staff, she was drafted in to judge the 100m sprint (possibly because they thought she could count). My co-competitor in Barra was one of the finalists and I guess he loosely fitted into the 'friend of the family' category. I hadn't managed to make the final so I stood beside my mum at the finish line to get the best possible view of the conclusion to the race. What followed was quite astonishing...

Sprints can often be pretty close-run things so you can excuse some initial confusion with the result. However, for my mum to award the race to someone who didn't even make the fucking photo is nothing short of professional negligence. School sports day events should always be decided on merit - not on who the judge happens to recognise from her son's birthday party.

Thankfully after a brief stewards' enquiry the race was retrospectively awarded to the guy who'd finished about ten yards in front of everyone else.

***

But let's get back to Barra. There was one member of our group that none of us really knew and we all wondered who had actually invited her. For the purposes of the book we'll call her '*Eileen*'...

Towards the end of our holiday, the gym hall radiators suddenly became festooned with *hunners** of pairs of blue flowery knickers. There were at least fifteen of them. I mean, come on Eileen - that's more than two weeks' worth of pants! It looked like they were all identical so presumably there'd been some sort of BOGOF/multibuy offer at the time.

One of the girls suggested that they might actually have been breeding, however no scientific or forensic evidence was ever found (unlike the hot dog sausages - more on that shortly…)

It transpired that 'Eileen' had been travelling solo in the highlands & islands for several weeks and this was the first place that had a washing machine and drying facilities. Fair enough I suppose. She must have been so lonely before arriving in Barra so we were delighted to be able to offer her friendship, warmth (and sausages).

Our 6 hour ferry journey back to Oban felt like 6 weeks but our 1984 Barra trip was one of the most enjoyable experiences of our teenage lives.

[**hunners**: any number between 3 and a billion]

It's only when you leave that you realise just what a special place it is. If I'm gonna be 500 miles from anywhere, I would always choose to be on a Scottish island. They are idyllic places where nothing ever happens, but just occasionally something does.

When we arrived back off the ferry, I had run out of cash and so had to get my guitar out and busk for my bus fare home to Glasgow.

As it turned out, I managed to complete the task within just five songs (probably because people wanted me to stop). Anyway, I happily boarded the single decker down the A85 reflecting that although it wasn't quite money for nothing, it was still a fairly straightforward way to fund your public transport home. In an effort to pass the time, I decided to try and formulate a mathematical equation to illustrate what had just taken place, and came up with:

Σ (2 * Simon & Garfunkel's)+(2 * Don McLean's) +(1 * Neil Diamond) = 70p

The Barra experience didn't end there though, as within a few weeks we'd been invited to Pollok

Police Headquarters for an interview. On the basis that none of us had applied for a job there, we started to get a bit worried...

Unbeknown to us, there had been a break-in at the schoolhouse after we'd left and so the Scottish polis needed to eliminate us from their enquiries. The ensuing scene could easily have made it on to any of the top TV cop dramas of the time. There were two officers present at the interview, one who made Jimmy Boyle look like Julian Clary and the other who could barely avoid giggling herself to death.

The bad cop opened with "*We'd like to talk to you about hot dog sausages*". Now as chat up lines go this was right up there, however the pure dourness of his demeanour nearly caused me to have a wee accident in the toilet department. You see as the main perp (and consumer), I knew I had to carry the can (quite literally). I was 19 and my adult life had barely begun. Police stations can be pretty scary places and although I didn't feel I'd committed a serious crime, you just never know how these things are going to play out. I had a horrible feeling that this might end up being a very cruel summer.

However after an agonising ten minutes or so we were released without charge - mainly thanks to the female cop needing to be helped up off the floor and resuscitated.

So I'm pleased to say that our Hebridean hullabaloo had a happy ending and we slipped quietly into our twenties without even a hint of a police record (other than *Synchronicity*). We'd thrown caution to the wind but without actually receiving a caution.

KARAOKE/KARAJOKIE
So I went to the doctors...

CHAPTER SIX

KARAOKE / KARAJOKIE

The end of the eighties marked the beginning of our passionate and enduring love affair with Karaoke. There's something about the Glasgow psyche that made this a perfect fit.

We have a natural modesty which can often result in some absolutely outstanding singers being 'accidentally' discovered as they genuinely have no idea how good they are. It also plays to our insatiable desire to *'gie it laldy'*. In fact Karaoke could have been invented just for Glaswegians. Whatever the reason it was (and still is) a fundamental part of Glasgow's weekend entertainment scene and there's one venue which will forever be synonymous with Karaoke in the city - *The Horseshoe Bar.*

Aside from having the longest bar servery in Europe (104 feet and three inches apparently), it also became the beating heart of Glasgow's new crooning craze and for many performers it was a fairly serious business. In fact some the more committed karaokers would have stage names (presumably to avoid too much unwanted attention from HMRC).

Around that time my (now) wife and I went to a friend's wedding and were amused to discover that the singer's name was *Ken Love.* Aye right Ken. Just a wee bit too convenient a name for a wedding singer? So I thought two can play at that game and the following weekend *Don Passion* burst on to the karaoke scene, and the rest (as they say) is mystery...

A number of my singing friends also came up with some memorable performing names like: *Neil the Deal, Vince Prince, Perry Mason* and my favourite, *Gary-oke.*

Perry Mason's real name was Patrick and he performed his renditions from his wheelchair. So his stage name was a very clever play on the fact that

Raymond Burr played the wheelchair bound *'Man Called Ironside'* which was then followed by his first (ahem) 'stand up' role as *Perry Mason.*

We arrived for a daytime session one Sunday afternoon to discover that there was a reporter there from *STV news* who was interviewing some of the regulars to understand why there had been such an explosion of interest in it. I managed to catch his eye and we had a good blether which concluded by him asking me whether *Don Passion* was my real name. I said "Don't be ridiculous, of course it's not. My real name is *George Passion*".

Sadly, this comedy gem was left on the cutting room floor as I presume there had been some real news that day.

The host at the Horseshoe was a guy called Jim who's catchphrase was *"Come on up and you could win a bottle of whisky or a bottle of vodka"*. I still get a bit tingly when I hear the shout: *"Don Passion, you're up next"*. The adrenaline used to pump like a big pumpy thing. Jim actually ended up hosting the Karaoke at our wedding (yes of course we had a singalong as part of the proceedings). He also snogged one of my work colleagues (although the two incidents are not thought to have been connected).

We even had Elvis perform at our wedding despite the fact that he had died fifteen years prior to our big day. *Neil the Deal* was an accomplished Elvis impersonator whose lush velvety voice was matched only by his designer sister's stitchwork. She created a shimmering white rhinestone suit for the occasion which '*The King*' himself would have been proud of. I can still remember his security detail rushing him in and out of the room to protect him from any overly hysterical aunties and uncles. Neil if you're listening, people still talk about the '*wonder of you*'.

***

There was a lesser known west-end venue just off Gibson Street called the *Blythswood Cottage* which had a slightly more relaxed approach to the whole karaoke thing. If you couldn't sing then you had the option to do kara-jokie, and if you couldn't tell a joke then you could just do the Hokey Cokey (ok I made that last bit up).

I always fancied myself as a bit of stand-up comedian and you might be surprised to hear that in the early part of my career I was compared to Billy Connolly. However unfortunately compared to Billy Connolly I was pish.

There was a fresh influx of audience every week at the *Cottage* and so you could almost get away with telling the same jokes. This was a theory that I tested to its absolute limit.

***

The Alpen Lodge sounds like the kind of place where an Orangeman might have his breakfast, however it was also what you might call a *'pre-karaoke'* venue. It was handily placed next to Central Station on Hope Street and had a guy with keyboard who could play anything in any key - which was just as well as the majority of the clientele would sing in H♭.

The slightly bizarre thing was that they all seemed to want to sing the same song. A lamentable ballad called *The Last Thing on My Mind*. The track was written by a bloke called Tom Paxton and was recorded by more than fifty artists including Dolly Parton, Glen Campbell and Chris de Burgh. (Note: it's not to be confused with the dance-pop floor filler of the same name performed by yet another famous Glasgow band called '*Stepps*'). Anyway the song is actually quite good. The opening line is:

It's a lesson too late for the learnin'
Made of sand, made of sand

The phrasing is relatively straightforward, however for some reason the local vocalists felt it could be improved by introducing a curious technique known as 'mid-syllable breathing' resulting in:

It's a le-hesson to lay-hate furra le-hearnin'
Made affa sa-hand, made affa sa-hand

I don't think that it was nerves or any particular respiratory condition, it just seemed to be how they liked to do things at the Lodge. Maybe they had just sprinted back from the bar to avoid missing their turn and were still getting their breath back.

The Alpen Lodge was also the place to go if you wanted a demonstration of Scottish yodelling. There had obviously been some sort of Austrian influence somewhere along the line or perhaps some of the punters had recently been 'high on a hill with a lonely goat herd'.

Scottish yodelling is a rare skill which was probably best demonstrated by Lanarkshire country & western legend *Sydney Devine* (or Steak & Kidney as he was affectionately known). His biggest chart hit was *Tiny Bubbles,* however his yodelling was best showcased in his glass-shattering live performances of *Crystal Chandeliers*.

I suspect Steak & Kidney had a significant influence on the Alpen Lodge faithful, as many of the acts included a touch of yodelling in their renditions. In fact there was so much yodelling went on that you could have quite legitimately renamed it the 'Alpine' Lodge.

I once went there with the intention of trying to impress a girlfriend with my singing capabilities. However not surprisingly I never got a turn as there were people there who had clearly been waiting for months. It's still open today, although I'm not sure whether you're still expected to split your syllables with every breath you take.

THE THREE CAPTAINS

CHAPTER SEVEN

THE THREE CAPTAINS

(BIRDSEYE, PUGWASH & SENSIBLE)

Ok stay with me here. I know the chapter title might seem a wee bit 'out there', however this section deals with three key elements of 1980s television:

1. The Adverts
2. Primetime TV programmes
3. Truly dreadful novelty pop hits...

A quick reminder that there was no internet in the 80s and no mobile phones either, so sticking on the TV or reading the newspapers was really the only way that you could find out what was going on. Although we did have *BBC Ceefax* which was a kind of pre-google way of catching up on the news and booking cheap holidays. However waiting for it to scroll through 173 pages took considerably longer than your actual holiday.

It was also pre-cable or satellite, so we were stuck with only three channels until the end of 1982 when *Channel Four* limped on to the scene. We were all expecting a dramatic and exhilarating countdown to the new channel's arrival on to our screens but instead we got …*Countdown.*

Although it was a fairly underwhelming start to things, it's now in its 93rd series and has broadcast more than 8,000 episodes. In fact its enduring success has been a bit of a 'conundrum' to many of us. I just hope I live long enough to see the final Countdown.

We should also remember that in those days there was no pause/fast forward option, so you were forced to watch all the adverts (or go and make a cup of *Tetley* or *Maxwell House).*

Our inability to skip through the commercials meant that the ads really did their job in those days.

The fact that we still remember so many of them is testament to that. Which tees us up very nicely for our first Captain - the jovial, nautical, candy-floss-couponed *Captain Birdseye* and his mouthwatering selection of frozen fish offerings. As a sign of the times, his fish fingers were 100% cod which would cost a bloody fortune these days. But only the best for the captain's table!

Clearly there was a time and a *plaice* for these adverts and Captain B was always the *lythe* and *sole* of the party when it came to TV commercials. I mean for *cod*'s *hake,* he was a national *fin*-stitution!

He never actually got paid apparently, he just did it for the *halibut*. Now I know you're probably starting to think what a load of *pollocks*. But don't worry I'm beginning to *flounder* now and to be honest I've *haddock* with all this fish pun nonsense.

However in my defence, it's hardly surprising that I have such a fishy focus when the two previous first ministers of Scotland were called *Salmon*d and *Sturgeon*.

There were some pretty fishy pop acts too like Feargal *Sharkey*, *Skate* Bush, *Marlin* Manson, Texas songwriting duo Johnny *Mackerel*hone and *Sardine* Spiteri, *Ray* Parker Jr., *Cod* Stewart, *Roach*ford, and last but not least - *Pike & Tuna* Turner. Oh and quite a few of the 80s pop stars had *mullets*...

Maybe it's just me, but the TV ads in the 80s seemed to have so much more impact than they do now. Today's ads tend to look a bit 'tired' - unlike the *Goodyear Grand Prix S* advert where Sir Robert Mark convinced us that they were a major contribution to road safety...and we believed him!

And for some strange reason there seemed to be an inordinate amount of tea adverts on the TV in the eighties. Mind you, pretty much everyone drank tea so I suppose the size of the target market justified it. In a highly competitive marketplace, the 'flakes' were high and the big brands left no 'leaf' unturned in order to 'bag' a larger share of the market.

Their marketing teams were clearly no 'mugs' and treated every new ad launch as their 'cup' final before everything went to 'pot'. In fact it all became a bit of a 'Brew-haha'.

Tetley continued to reinforce the Yorkshire stereotype and promoted the idea that having 2000 perforations was a critical component to creating the perfect cuppa.

Shortly afterwards, we saw what can only be described as a seismic shift in the global hot beverage market with the introduction of the *round* tea bag. I mean, Jeezo - I feel like I've only just recovered!

PG Tips had the most immaculately trained chimps on the planet and always delivered the most laughs although "You only get an *'oo'* with *Typhoo*" probably had the catchiest slogan.

And who can forget *Brooke Bond* Dividend Tea (*a cup of D*) which continued to play the discount card by offering us redeemable coupons (although not the face type).

So even if the TV adverts weren't everybody's 'cup of tea', we continued to drink plenty of the stuff. I'll move on to the Scottish TV adverts shortly, but just to complete the picture on a more national level who could forget:

- ***Hamlet*** with the future Rab C Nesbitt (Gregor Fisher) struggling with his comb-over in a photo booth.

- The ***Milky Bar Kid*** (who by that stage had a beard and three kids).

- ***Brut 33*** began to lose its allure in the 1980s as nobody wanted to smell like their uncle.

- For **Mash get *Smash*** (complete with giggling robot aliens ripping the absolute pish out of us humans)

- ***Um Bongo,*** *Um Bongo* they drink it in the Congo (…and in Govan apparently)

- We were queueing up with our hoovers to *"do the **Shake n' Vac** and put the freshness back"* ♫

- ***Cinzano Bianco*** with Reggie Perrin and Joan Collins convincing us it was still the suavest of swallies.

- The tear jerking ***Yellow Pages*** classic where JR Hartley eventually manages to find a copy of his own book

Oh, and the ***Milk Tray*** guy was still diving off cliffs to deliver a box of chocolate coated excitement to a mysterious woman with nice hands.

Although we all continued to be charmed by these national ad treasures, back in Scotland they were interspersed with some more local offerings which featured some of these timeless classics:

- ***Knorr Stock Cubes*** had the ability to produce pea & ham from a chicken. Now that's clever!
- ***Irn Bru*** made in Scotland from 'Gurdurzz'!
- ***STERLING*** Tillicoultry, near Stirling (but not that near). You certainly wouldn't want to try and walk it if you were carrying a sofa.
- There's always change at ***Agnews!*** (but not now that we have minimum alcohol pricing)
- Buzz into ***Behar Carpets*** and you'll never get 'stung' with our prices. Oh beehave…

- ***Glens, Hutchison, Robertsons & Stepek*** were the 'pre-Comet' go-to guys for all your white goods. What a brilliant idea it was for four local independent electrical retailers to club together to save money on TV advertising! Yet another fine example of Scottish innovation.

***

But let's move on to our second seafaring superstar, the pompous and preposterous *Captain Pugwash* and his band of blundering buffoons. I feel I have to start by debunking a myth…

I know that many people of my generation will be utterly heartbroken to learn that there weren't actually any vulgar or smutty character names in the iconic maritime cartoon series. Of course we all wish there had been, but sadly it was all just a figment of our filthy teenage imagination.

There was even a court case about it which proved beyond doubt that there was never a *Master Bates,* nor a *Seaman Staines* and definitely no *Roger the Cabin Boy* (although there was a cabin boy however unfortunately his name was Tom). Ah well, we can always pretend…

But it did have an extremely catchy accordion theme tune which if you're a ceilidh fan is the perfect accompaniment to a *Canadian Barn Dance.*

To be honest, I'd grown out of Captain P by the time the 80s came along and I'd started focusing my attention on something a little bit more grown up-ish. Fortunately, there was some pretty decent stuff on the box around that time like:

- Hitch Hikers Guide to the Galaxy
- Auf Wiedersehen, Pet
- Magnum P.I.
- Allo, Allo!
- The A-Team
- Baywatch
- Hart to Hart
- Only Fools & Horses
- Minder
- Not the Nine O'clock News
- The Young Ones
- Blackadder (…the best of the lot I think)

North of the border we had *Superscot, Supergran* and the classic eighties Glasgow restaurant starter choice: *Soup or Orange Juice.*

But fortunately Scottish TV became known for something a whole lot better...

TAGGART ran for nearly thirty years and pretty much every Scottish actor worth their salt (& vinegar) got a part in it at some point in their career. The acting wasn't quite Oscar quality but the gritty storylines were superb and it became an unmissable part of the weekly schedule. In fact *Taggart* almost became a religion. Well, kind of. Let me explain...

When we were getting married, part of the deal if you wanted to do the deed in a catholic church was that you had to get a form signed confirming that you'd both received *'religious instruction'* around (ahem) well, you know - that stuff...

Fortunately, I knew a guy at university who had recently become a priest and he seemed like the safest (and cheapest) bet. So we invited him round to the flat one evening to sign our pink slip and tell us nothing that we didn't already know. He arrived half an hour late, burst into the sitting room and said:

"*Taggart*'s on, have you got any wine big man?" As soon as *Taggart* (and all the wine) was finished he resurrected himself from the couch, picked up his cassock and holy spirited himself back to Shettleston. Thankfully he had left our signed marriage permit sitting safely on the coffee table (presumably filled in during the adverts).

Bless you father....

***

And finally we move on to Captain number three, the '*Damned*' delightful *Captain Sensible.* Raymond Burns was a new-wave pioneer who stuck on a red beret and John Lennon sunglasses to sing a song from a 1949 Rogers & Hammerstein Musical. Hmm, perhaps not quite what we would have expected from a punk rocker.

But after us recovering from the shock of Joe Dolce's 'Shaddap You Face' keeping Ultravox's 'Vienna' off the top of the charts the previous year, we should have known that there were more nasty novelty surprises to come. But poor Midge. When he was asked about being robbed of the top spot by a mandolin playing actor in leather trousers he said: *"This means nothing to me ♪♪"*. But I'm sure it meant plenty to him...

Anyway, It's more than a bit of an embarrassment to say I remember this lot:

Renee and Renato

Save Your Love

The Four Bucketeers

The Bucket of Water Song

Chas & Dave (with the Matchroom Mob)

Snooker Loopy

Kenny Everett

Snot Rap

The Brat

Chalk Dust - The Umpire Strikes Back

The Firm

Star Trekkin' and Arthur Daley E's Alright

Weird Al Yankovic

Eat It (which was a parody of Wacko Jacko's Beat it)

The Commentators

N-N-Nineteen Not Out (which was a parody of Paul Hardcastle's 19)

Alexei Sayle

Ullo John! Gotta New Motor? (a parody of cockney chants)

Spitting Image

The Chicken Song (a parody of all the dreadful Black Lace numbers)

I'm not sure that I considered these 'novelty' records when they came out. They were just songs on *Top of the Pops*. Perhaps there were so many of them that it all just got normalised and there was nothing we could 'Agadoo' about it.

Video Cassette Recorders (VCRs) started to become affordable in the 80s and Sony & JVC began fighting for their share of a rapidly growing market.

As we know, the sun always shines on TV and being able to capture that was seen as a technological *tour de force*. And while Sony's *Betamax* was always the superior technology, *VHS* ultimately won the format fight due to their longer recording times and (eventually) more affordable prices. The *VHS* versus *Betamax* battle is still cited today as a cautionary tale to illustrate that the best product doesn't always win.

VCRs were somewhat life changing for many of us as you no longer had to plan your life around the TV schedule. You could happily go out on the *randan** safe in the knowledge that you could watch your favourite TV show when you got back (unless of course some tube had recorded over it).

I thought at this point I might be lamenting that video killed the radio star. But surprisingly enough it didn't…

[**randan**: a bevvy session]

The Union

CHAPTER EIGHT

THE UNION

Glasgow University Union (GUU) was a huge part of my life during the 1980s. My Mum & Dad had met at Glasgow Uni in the late 50s and my brother and I were students there at the same time. I was going to say 'studied there' at the same time but that wouldn't be entirely accurate…

In my first year I took maths, statistics and computing science which was largely fine until the sums got a bit too hard. I had started spending a bit more time at the GUU as that was the most obvious place to meet up with your pals who were studying different subjects.

My Dad had been on the Union board when he did his law degree and he hung around with some pretty interesting people - many of whom became lifelong friends. That fact clearly had a subconscious influence as I found myself standing for election to the GUU board in my second year and stayed on until I completed my term as President in 1988.

I ended up living at Gilmorehill on a semi-permanent basis, as the board members had access to free overnight accommodation when they were on duty. That turned out to be a very handy perk.

My guitar lived with me at the Union and tended to travel with me wherever I went. At least that was until one of my fellow board members* managed to demolish it during a poorly performed gymnastics routine. His failed attempt to vault over the couch resulted in his fairly sizeable *Olga Kor*-butt flattening my pride and joy. It meant that I was left temporarily instrumentless until we could organise a replacement via the Union's insurance policy.

*(*The culprit shall remain anonymous except to say he's about 5ft 9 with short dark hair, always wears a kilt and has a beard like a rhododendron bush).*

During those dark days (it was winter to be fair), I discovered that there was an old upright piano at the back of the debating hall and quickly found out that guitar chords worked pretty well on the keys, as long as you had big hands and could add in some twiddly bits here and there.

So I ended up being more of a pianoman than a guitarist although I'd clearly not thought it through very well - as trying to carry a piano up to someone's fourth floor flat for a party was a bit of a non-starter. However that didn't really hold me back too much as most of my performing was done at the Union. The GUU had a huge number of affiliated clubs & societies, so there would often be some sort of social event going on which would inevitably descend into a load of drunken students wanting to have a sing song. I never needed a second invitation. However I always made sure I followed one golden rule which is best represented by the following set of statements:

=IF [# of drinks consumed by performer] EQUALS LESS THAN [# of drinks consumed by audience] THEN = (performance goes well)

And conversely:

=IF ([# of drinks consumed by performer] EQUALS MORE THAN [# of drinks consumed by audience] THEN = (performer gets booed off)

So the key lesson was always ensure that the audience is a couple of drinks ahead of you and you can't go wrong.

Having grown up with *Morecambe & Wise* and *The Two Ronnies* (not literally of course as social services might have been involved), I was always a fan of the comedy song. I suspect that Richard Stilgoe and Victoria Wood also had a bit of an influence on me as I started to get quite into rewriting the lyrics to well-known tunes to help feed my insatiable craving for an audience. I started to road-test my humorous piano parodies at Union Debates where there was always a slot in proceedings for letting your hair down (and to be fair there was quite a lot of hair around in the 80s).

These less serious interludes were known as 'stunts' and with a bit of creativity, you could quite easily turn the theme of the day into some sort of pithy musical satire. I was never a particularly good debater, but I loved performing and I was always willing to risk making a complete arse of myself.

Glasgow University has an exceptional record in international debating circles and the GUU are five time winners of the *World Universities Debating Championship* (WUDC) and 16-time champions of *The John Smith Memorial Mace* (previously known as the *Observer Mace* until 1995). It's incredibly fitting that the competition title was changed to honour the memory of our most famous Convener of Debates who many still regard as the best Prime Minister the UK never had.

The Union has a fabulous Debates Chamber which spans two floors of the historic Gilmorehill building and many of our most famous politicians and business leaders honed their craft there. I can't begin to do any sort of justice to the Union's debating pedigree, so I'll leave that to someone who can.

My second term on the Union board was from 1985-86 as Convener of Games. This was much more up my street (or so I thought…)

The GUU Snooker Hall was one of the best in the country and in those days had twelve full-sized tables. It was always mobbed and there were weekly competitions where the winners received 'beer chits' which could be exchanged for free pints in the beer bar. It resulted in the Union putting together a pretty formidable league team.

As Convener, I was entrusted with the keys to the Snooker Hall which not surprisingly resulted in the occasional all-nighter. I remember after one of them, bravely appearing at my 9am Statistics lecture and managing to fall asleep while the lecturer was staring right at me. What was the probability of that happening? It was very nearly my last roll of the dice...

However my 'big bet' of the year was to organise a darts exhibition match featuring Jocky Wilson and Eric Bristow. Jocky had won the World Championship two years earlier and was a national hero. His celebrity status was only enhanced when his chubby coupon appeared as the backdrop to *Dexy's Midnight Runners* live performance of 'Jackie Wilson Said' on Top of the Pops.

We all wanted to believe it had been a terrible blunder by the BBC, however like many urban myths all wasn't quite what it seemed. Kevin Rowland admitted that he'd just done it for a laugh because nobody would have been stupid enough to believe it was a genuine mistake. Apart from Radio One DJ Mike Read who said on his show the next morning: *"How could Top of the Pops mix up a legendary soul singer with a Scottish darts player?"*

Jocky's opponent on the night was supposed to be *'The Crafty Cockney'* who at that time was the world number one. However, a few days before the event he'd clearly received a much better offer as he was unexpectedly subbed by Cliff Lazarenko. To be fair *'Big Cliff'* was also a pretty big draw, but just not as big as Eric unfortunately and we finished up with a slightly under capacity crowd of about 23.

So to cut a long story short my signature event as Convener of Games was an abject failure of fairly momentous proportions. A fiascotic debacle. But you can't win them all and at least it helped me rule out marketing & events as a career choice. But thankfully darts wasn't the only game in town...

The 1980s was also the decade when arcade video games really started to take hold. The Union had a fantastic selection next to the beer bar which were regularly refreshed with the very latest offerings. We also had some of the best pinball machines of the era and the games room was always a hive of flashing lights and plonky noises. The early eighties arcade video games like *Space Invaders, Asteroids, Defender* and *Missile Command* had started to make way for some equally addictive newcomers which included legends like:

- *Pac-Man*
- *Super Mario Brothers*
- *Spy Hunter*
- *Hyper Sports / Track & Field*
- *Pole Position*

The more committed/obsessed players would often end up with variety of repetitive strain injuries due to overly vigorous hand & wrist movements, which was an awkward thing to have to explain to your parents/girlfriend.

As an officially registered members' club, we were also licensed to put large jackpot fruit machines in all the bar areas. The prospect of winning £100 on the puggy in 1984 was a serious draw and I have to admit that I often played slightly beyond my student budget. It was only when I got to look at the Union accounts that I appreciated why so many members clubs signed up for the one-armed bastards (sorry bandits). Those machines made an absolute bloody fortune!

I got my own back forty years later when I acquired an old puggy for the house and was able to keep all the takings for myself. However, I stupidly located it in the conservatory and it melted during the unusually roasting summer of 2022.

DAFT FRIDAY

One of the really nice things about being President of the Union is that the annual *Daft Friday Ball* is themed in your honour. The tradition was that it had to be some kind of play on your surname and I ended up with *Don Magloglione*. So it had a kind of 1920s mafia gangster-esque theme to it with lots of clandestine speakeasys and dimply lit gangland gathering spots.

The DF Ball always managed to land some pretty impressive bands and the headline act would perform to a euphoric crowd in the two-tier Debates Chamber. In previous years we'd had groups like: *Lindisfarne, Thin Lizzy, The Boomtown Rats* and the beehive-haired *Mari Wilson.*

But it was *Runrig* who were just what I always wanted, and we were delighted when they agreed to perform. The Celtic rockers were just reaching the peak of their success in 1987, with their fifth album *The Cutter and the Clan* getting released just a few weeks before their gig at the Union.

They blew the place away with their roof raising performance of 'Loch Lomond', but it was another song which ended up being a very personal highlight for me. When they got to my favourite Runrig rock ballad (*Going Home*), their charismatic frontman Donnie Munro said: "This one's for you Donald". I cried like a baby…

It wouldn't have been University life if there hadn't been the odd 'student prank' here and there.

We managed to introduce quite a few to our list, including:

- 'Borrowing' an enormous plant pot from the Hilton Hotel in the back of a taxi and leaving it gracing the front steps to the Union. Well done to the driver for agreeing to it (although we didn't give him much option). The hotel collected it a couple of days later using their own transport and were surprisingly understanding about the whole affair.

- Singing *'The Laughing Policeman'* on the roof of a bus shelter at 6.30am (whilst wearing a kilt) and then being asked to explain myself to a couple of bemused passing police officers. My explanation was that I had just left Daft Friday (hence the kilt), and that the early Saturday morning commuters seemed to be enjoying it (in fact some of them had started to ask for requests). I'm not sure the cops actually bought my explanation, but fortunately there had been some slightly more serious crimes taking place in Glasgow that weekend so I was let off with a slightly bewildered warning. I always wondered if either of them reflected on the irony of my song choice…

- Taking a comatosely blootered visiting Oxford student (while still in his bed) and relocating him (and the bed) on to a traffic island outside the Union so that he would wake up with a surprise the next morning. The passing traffic also seemed to get a bit of a surprise. Happily he was brought back to life without incident and the now (fairly well known) former Oxbridge undergraduate can see the funny side. I know I can!

- Photocopying your arse. Now I'll admit that's something that most people have probably done, however the copier machine we had at the Union was so old that it was actually the glass screen that moved across to capture the image (rather than the camera) and this resulted in the edge of the glass panel slicing through somebody's ball sack (mid-copy). However fortunately there was a partially trained medical student on hand who had a needle & thread and an eye for detail. It was reassuring for us to know that if we had needed to involve the emergency services then at least we would have had some helpful photos for them to look at.

- Kilted chair-jumping events whereby you ran across the Reading Room, did a quick half-turn in mid-air while vaulting over several chair-based obstacles and then landed safely (bum first) on one of the leather chesterfields. Wearing a kilt was compulsory (even for the women). We even had a few celebrity participants over the years.

- And finally, I would love to claim that the now well established tradition of sticking a traffic cone on top of the Duke of Wellington's statue was started by me. But it wasn't. However, it might have been started by one of my pals, as several of them claimed to have done it at some point in the early eighties. So even if they weren't actually the first, it's possible that they might have been one of the first (maybe).

One of the really useful things about being on the Union board as a student was that you learned quite a lot about how small businesses worked.

I remember one of the surprising revelations being that even a very minor adjustment to the size of a portion of baked beans could have a significant impact on the overall profit of the catering operation. Once I'd got 'wind' of this, I did briefly consider a career as a 'bean counter'.

However by that stage it was becoming fairly clear that I wasn't going to excel academically, so I decided to just make the most of the extra-curricular side of university life. Thankfully that decision paid off as I managed to secure my first job through my Union connections and I continued to benefit from those relationships throughout my working life.

I cut my teeth on after dinner speaking while I was there which turned out to be a really useful skill to take into my sales & business career. I remember years later being introduced as a 'seasoned public speaker'. I thought, I'll take that as a condiment!

The final experience that the Union provided was slightly more unexpected. The chance to make my first (and very nearly second) TV appearance. The Head of Features at *BBC Scotland* had been the producer of a programme called '*Open to Question*' which in the early 80s provided groups of school kids with the opportunity to interrogate some key public figures like: Arthur Scargill, Desmond Tutu, Jeffrey Archer, Billy Connolly and Princess Anne.

So as a producer he'd had experience working with children and animals and so he decided to capitalise on the Union's global debating successes by commissioning a series called '*A House Divided*'.

It was a televised debating competition which included Oxbridge and some of the other ancient universities like Edinburgh and St. Andrews. It was pretty cool to have a BBC Scotland Outside Broadcast Team camped out in the Union for a week. I landed the job of marching in with a big mace and shouting "*Hats off strangers*!" Ok, so it wasn't quite a '*De Niro*' moment but I'll take it.

My (nearly) second TV appearance was as a contestant on the regional pre-selection for *University Challenge*. I think I only got one answer correct but it was a belter...

The question was:

Who said, "If I'm going to be a woman Geoffrey I'll need to have a bosom"?

I nearly broke my buzzer when I blurted in with:

"Was it Bungle from Rainbow?"

Of course it was. Ten points to us plus three bonus questions worth five points each…

However, in a quite astonishing travesty of justice, I wasn't selected to be in the final Glasgow University team for the main BBC televised programme. I can only presume that they thought my specialist areas of knowledge were just a bit too 'niche'.

***

A few years after I finished my term on the GUU board, I bumped into the former Union Manager and he invited me for a round of golf at Glasgow Gailes links. Now there was an invite I wasn't going to turn down. Gailes is very much in the same league as Troon and Turnberry and has been a British Open Championship qualifying venue for fifty plus years.

He suggested I arrive around midday so that we could enjoy a couple of pints before teeing it up at 1pm. In hindsight, I should probably have eaten some breakfast, as by the time I got on to the first tee I have to admit I felt a wee bit squiffy. The next thing I knew, I'd hit a very high slice which started to make its way towards the car park. Oh dear…

I winced as I waited for the sound of smashing glass but instead there was just a very loud thud. What happened next will sound like one of those peculiar dream sequences where your auntie Flora suddenly appears wearing a diving helmet.

What actually happened next was that the *Alexander Brothers* appeared. It turned out that Tom & Jack were teeing off in the group behind us. The tartan folk singing siblings were a kind of 1960s version of the Proclaimers (but just much funnier). They had learned their trade in the old music halls so they knew how to work an audience. I asked them if they'd seen or heard anything of the incident - to which Jack replied, *"Oh my god what a dunt it made!"*

Shit. It would have been just my luck for it to have landed on some posh guy's Bentley. *"Oh don't worry pal"* Jack added, *"I think it was a purple Allegro".*

Now I'd been working for a few years by then and had bought myself a (purplish) grey *Vauxhall Calibra,* which was a kind of low budget, sporty-ish hatchback. But it didn't look anything like an *Austin Allegro*. In fact I don't think I had seen an *Allegro* of any colour in fifteen years.

So it transpired that within a golf club car park containing maybe a hundred or so prestige cars, I'd managed to hit my own.

I mean seriously...What were the chances? It would have been easier for me to have got a hole-in-one using an umbrella whilst playing the bagpipes.

However it wasn't all bad, as the cost of the bodywork repair and respray to the front wing was partially offset by the £50 prize I won for letter of the month in BBC's *Top Gear Magazine*. Every cloud and all that...(although nobody likes to start their round with a seven at the first).

Being on the Union Board was definitely one of those life-shaping experiences - made even 'shapier' by the fact that it took place right in the middle of what was an unforgettable decade for Scottish pop music. I feel extremely lucky to have had a similarly enriching experience to my Mum & Dad and that I'm still in close touch with many of the amazing people I met at the GUU forty years ago.

Scottish Movie Magic

CHAPTER NINE

SCOTTISH MOVIE MAGIC

The eighties was also a golden decade for Scottish filmmaking. We punched well above our weight on the global stage and created some enduring comedy classics. The best of the bunch had to be *Gregory's Girl* which was directed by Bill Forsyth. As *'coming of age'* romcoms go, this was as good as it got. A clumsy, awkward, gangly teenager trying to cop off with the only girl in the school football team and then ending up snogging her pal. It could have been any of us.

It also created one of the great pub quiz 'trick' questions: "Who was Gregory's Girl?" It wasn't Dee Hepburn (even though she was the one that featured on the movie poster). The real Gregory's girl was Susan, played by Clare Grogan from Altered Images. I could be happy to watch their dancing-lying-down scene again and again.

Chic Murray was outstanding as the grumpy old headmaster and Jake D'Arcy played a blinder as Mr. Menzies the glaikit PE teacher.

The standout scene was their poker-faced exchange around the film's most thorny issue...

[Headmaster] *There's a girl in the football team?*

[PE teacher] *Well yes and no...well yes.*

[Headmaster] *What do you mean?*

[PE teacher] *Well we could have girl in the football team if we wanted one.*

[Headmaster] *Do we want one*?

[PE teacher, hesitantly] *Well.....*

[Headmaster] *I think it's a wonderful idea. Terrific!*

[PE teacher] *Yes, and she's a great wee player. She won't hold the team back one little bit!*

[Headmaster] *One possible problem area. The showers. What happens about the showers?*

[PE teacher] *Oh - she'll bring her own soap!*

Many of the other classic lines from the film are still heard around Glasgow today:

- If I don't see you through the week I'll see you through a window!
- Don't touch the ravioli it's garbage.
- Act your age. Away and break some windows.
- That's a dead loss son, go and get changed.
- Twelve tons of cornflakes pass under here every day. It's a well-known fact!
- Tits, bum, fanny - the lot.
- Off you go you small boys!
- Christ you're worse that my dad. He's old, at least he's got an excuse for being a prick!
- Parliamo Italiano? Nah, no really. Just bella, bella.

The film is enduringly charming and almost timeless (if you ignore the big hair). Many of the scenes feel like an explosion in a hormone factory and you just can't help feeling sorry for the gawky and gormless Gregory, especially as his pals were a bunch of pure diddies.

The film does a marvellous job of reinforcing something we've all known for a long time. Girls are so much more mature than boys at school. This fact is expertly exploited by Forsyth to the point where many of the scenes in the film are positively heaving with uncomfortable emotional chaos. The comedy isn't very complex, but it's brilliantly delivered. Like when the cringingly hopeless Mr. Menzies shares his insightful assessment of the two basic skills required of a goalscorer: "Ball control, shooting accuracy, and the ability to read the game." However he needn't have bothered, as the talent on display was about as noticeable as his two-day old moustache. Or at least until Dorothy arrived…

The final scene which will remain forever etched in my mind is when Dorothy scores a goal and the whole of the opposing team then queue up to hug her as well.

***

Local Hero brought Bill Forsyth together with the legendary movie producer David Puttnam, who helped recruit a piece of cinematic royalty. The hoary Hollywood heartthrob, Burt Lancaster.

More of a comedy-drama than a comedy, it shared the story of a Texan oil executive who is sent to a remote Scottish village to buy the place out so that he can build a refinery. However he gets wooed by the beautifulness of Scotland (obviously), and ends up questioning the whole capitalist philosophy. Then after getting spellbound by the splendour of the northern lights, the Houston hot shots end up agreeing to fund a research institute instead and they all live happily ever after.

It's no secret that all Americans love Scotland and the movie plays on that premise incessantly with some slightly over-exaggerated stereotyping. But it's all so expertly delivered that it's ultimately a very satisfying and heartwarming watch. There are some delightfully memorable moments like when the local hotelier (played by Denis Lawson from Star Wars), serves up *casserole de lapin* which has been prepared using the injured rabbit that Peter Riegert and Peter Capaldi had adopted as a pet after running over it earlier that day.

The film was a *'slam-dunk'* for Scottish tourism as it featured some of our most spectacular scenery like the picturesque white sands of Morar and an adorable little Aberdeenshire village called Pennan which was home to the red phone box on the movie poster. It also had a soundtrack by *Dire McStraits.*

***

Comfort & Joy was another Bill Forsyth cult classic. Who else could have got away with having an ice cream war hardman describe himself as *"Mr. Bunny, formerly Mr. Softy"* and keep a straight face. Although we didn't know it at the time, the former Mr Softy (Alex Norton) would become a future DCI Taggart.

The main character was Radio DJ Alan *'Dickie'* Bird, whose kleptomaniac girlfriend leaves him the weekend before Christmas. Although his heart had been stolen too, he throws himself into his work and cruises around a dark and rainy Glasgow in a red convertible BMW 323i (which in those days was rarer than a live haggis). He spots an attractive girl in the back of an ice-cream van (Clare Grogan from *Altered Images* again), and follows the van to its next stop off. He buys a 99 and a bar of McCowan's highland toffee before shelving any ideas of chatting her up due to Mr. Bunny cramping his style. A few moments later, he witnesses a violent attack on the van and starts to get gradually more embroiled in a bitter turf war between two rival Italian families. The film taught us all a valuable lesson in violent combat. If you're ever attacked with a baseball bat then your best form of defence is raspberry sauce.

***

The final one on my list of eighties Scottish movie classics is *Restless Natives*. This wasn't actually a Bill Forsyth film, although it felt like it could have been.

Ronnie works in an Edinburgh Joke Shop (a kind of east coast Tam Shepherds I suppose), and Will is between jobs. They transform themselves into the Clown and the Wolfman and use a toy puffer gun to rob coach loads of bemused American tourists in the highlands.

They escape on their bright red Suzuki GP 125 motorbike before showboating around the streets of the capital. They quickly become a media sensation, with tourists queueing around the block to have the privilege of being dispossessed by the dynamic duo.

However, Will the Wolfman starts to lose his nerve as he falls hopelessly in love with the female tour guide. But rather than pulling the plug on their crowd-pleasing capers, they decide to start sharing the proceeds with the local unemployed community which only serves to elevate their global celebrity status. And due to the massively positive impact the whole affair has had on Scottish tourism, the powers at be help them fake their own deaths and the three of them ride off into the sunset.

The most memorable scene is when Ronnie & Will are back in the joke shop gathering newspaper cuttings of their infamy. A policeman walks in and they think they've been rumbled. But after browsing sheepishly around the shop for a few moments the cop approaches the till…

[Policeman] *Do you have you any false tits?*

[Ronnie] *Oh.....aye!*

[Policeman] *How much are they?*

[Ronnie] *Eh - medium £4.75, large £6.50.*

[Policeman] *Medium. Could you eh, wrap them up?*

The film had a soundtrack by Big Country which just added to the whole Scottishness of the movie and it's recently been re-released as a stage musical.

***

The 1980s also saw *Highlander* hit our screens which featured a very handsome French guy (Christopher Lambert) and an even handsomer Scottish guy (Sean Connery). The plot was centred around ancient warriors cutting each other's heads off with big swords. The iconic line from the movie was:

> *"There can be only one!"*

However they've recently started shooting a remake with Henry Cavill which means that there will now be erm...two.

All of these big screen blockbusters happened long before *Braveheart* and *Trainspotting,* but they clearly did an excellent job of whetting the global appetite for what was to come…

A Fan of the Scran
Ubiquitous Chip
Today's Specials
12noon - £6.00
33pm - £6.00
35pm - £8.00

CHAPTER TEN

A FAN OF THE SCRAN

I like food. A lot. Like I mean a really big lot. In fact it's always on my mind. Fortunately I'm not alone.

Glasgow has always had a very strong foodie culture and we have produced some of the most respected chefs in the world (not all of whom swear). We also had some seriously good top-end eighties eateries like:

- *The Ubiquitous Chip*
- *The Rogano Oyster Bar*
- *The Buttery*
- *The Belfry*

- *The Malmaison*
- *The Fountain*
- *The Loon Fung*
- *Café Gandolfi*
- *La Fourchette*
- *La Bavarde* (owned by my pal's dad)
- *L'Ariosto* (now called the Barolo and popular for its live music & dancing)

We were also spoilt for choice with some amazing Indian restaurants like the *Shalimar,* the *Shish Mahal,* the *Kooh-I-Noor* and the *Ashoka.*

The *Shalimar* on Gibson Street was one of the first of the Glasgow curry houses to offer the 'All You Can Eat Indian Buffet'. A marketing masterstroke when you're situated smack bang in the middle of student land. However it resulted in some clarification being provided after one of my friends was carried out of the premises after over-currying himself into a food coma. The restaurant owner politely reminded him that for £4.95 it was "*Eat as much as you want*" not "*as much as you can*".

The *Shalimar* was directly across the road from *The Spaghetti Factory* which is where *Gregory's Girl* was waitressing when she was discovered by Bill Forsyth. It then became The *Boston Pizza Precinct* in the mid-eighties and is now the home of *Stravaigan* (which does a brilliant *Nasi Goreng* breakfast).

As the eighties wasn't a decade when many of us had much spare cash, finding inexpensive fast food was essential (especially at three o'clock in the morning when you were hungry like the wolf).

Goodies take-away on Great Western Road was the perfect culinary conclusion to a night on the batter and they knew exactly how to stimulate the Glasgow palate. Their donner kebab sauce was hotter than *Hot Lips Houlihan*'s hotpants (and even more so the next day). It certainly had your senses working overtime.

Why is it that take-away food always seems to taste so much better the next day? Even though you've watched it slowly congeal on the worktop, it's almost impossible not to be tempted. And living on a student budget meant that you had *to squeeze* every last drop of nourishment from your weekly food investment which led to some extremely innovative concoctions like: *Rock hard pizza crust served with sliced curry sauce and a mould reduction.*

***

The *Canton Express* was a late night Chinese fast-food place in Sauchiehall Street which quickly became the 'go to' end of the night nosh-stop before you poured yourself into a taxi. It also became home to another great example of opportunistic Glasgow visual humour. It had one of those big black menu boards with detachable white letters which could be switched around for amusement and confusion.

So their signature dish of SINGAPORE FRIED RICE/NOODLE quickly became SINGARPIO FREE NICE DOODLER*, and the exceptionally patient and understanding staff seemed perfectly happy for you to order exactly that. *(* Don't worry, I had to check the anagramming accuracy too…)*

However I always felt there was scope to be a little bit more adventurous with the letter mixing, particularly on the back of *Fawlty Towers* who had managed to create things like: *Fatty Owls, Watery Fowls, Farty Towels* and *Flowery Twats* - which was pretty impressive with a relatively limited number of letters to play with. However I never managed to produce anything more creative as it was always far too late at night for something so mentally taxing.

They were open till 4am and were located directly across the road from the Garage nightclub, so you can just imagine the kind of state some people were in when they sat down with their chopsticks.

I always wondered what the food would taste like if you were sober, or whether the menu had been specifically created for the blootered. It was the sort of restaurant where you could easily envisage them breathalysing you on the way in and if you weren't completely stocious they would politely redirect you to the nearest fish & chip shop.

The one thing everyone remembers about the *Canton Express* was how far away the toilets were. It was at least a mile and a half and involved lots of different staircases which would have been a big enough challenge to negotiate when you were sober.

There were at least a couple of reports of people who went for a 'single fish' and were never seen again...

The staff there must have undergone special training in how to deal with rubber people as they had the patience of angels. Although I did once hear about someone being hit with a ladle.

But let's move on from the ridiculous to the sublime and take a stroll down *Ashton Lane* which remains one of the most popular socialising spaces in the city. Its cobbled street can only be about fifty yards long but even in the 80s was able to cram in some pretty cool places to hang out. In those days its anchor tenants were the *Ubiquitous Chip, Cul De Sac,* the *Grosvener Café* and the *Ashoka.*

***

The Ubiquitous Chip is a cultural icon and has always represented the essence of Glasgow's gastronomic innovation & ambition.

Ronnie Clydesdale was a culinary pioneer and he brought a whole new dimension to the way Glaswegians ate. He had one vision and he stuck to it religiously. There was never any *gimme, gimme, gimme fried chicken* for Ronnie (or any chips for that matter), and he steered the way in the Glasgow food scene for nearly forty years until he died in 2010.

I was lucky enough to go to the 'Chip' a few times with my family during the eighties, mainly for birthday dinners and Burns Suppers. It just felt really special and unmistakably Scottish. The wine list was outstanding and they created freshly handwritten menus every single day which detailed the exact provenance of everything they had on offer like: *Loch Melfort Mussels, Shetland Cod, Scrabster landed scallops* and *Newtonmore Venison.* We always asked to get a table in the courtyard as it had a pond with real koi carp in it. There was also lots of greenery and foliage around and so you felt like you were in some kind of Glaswegian rainforest. Even more amazing were the Alasdair Gray murals - one at the pond and another on your way up the stairs to the brasserie.

The Burns Suppers were outstanding as they had real actors and professional pipers performing. There was a father and daughter playing there one year and it was the first time I'd ever heard a bagpipe harmony. It was haunting and mesmeric. The haggis was outstandingly good and the whole experience felt magical.

It was just one of those unique places in the 80s and I'm reliably reassured that its iconic features will still be there when it reopens after a recent multi-million pound refurb. Hopefully it will continue to be one the few places in the world where people come for lunch and end up staying for dinner.

French culture was a relatively new thing in Glasgow in the 1980s and for some it was a wee bit of a shock to the system to have something quite so exotic on your doorstep. I remember when some of the local cafés started selling croissants, the locals would ask for a 'hot curly bun'.

Cul de Sac was a crêperie with a bar upstairs, both of which were excellent. My favourite was their pear & stilton crêpe which went down brilliantly with a pint of Stella. It occupied the prime spot on the corner as you walked down from the university and was a really popular haunt for students in the mid-eighties.

The Grosvener Café was another stalwart of the original Ashton Lane scene and is thought to have been the first commercial venture to set its stall out on the cobbles. They served amazing Danish pastries and it was full of aspiring pop stars and blethering undergraduates.

We also had the iconic *Grosvener Cinema* in the lane which remains the oldest picture house in the city. In the early 80s it underwent a massive refurb and started the trend of the much plusher movie venue where you could take in a bottle of wine and make a real occasion of it.

Prior to the refurb, the cinema occupied the entire building, as opposed to just the ground floor as it is today. Towards the end of the 1980s, it started showing full audience participation screenings of *The Rocky Horror Picture Show* - including theatre scrubs, fishnet stockings and lots of shouting out and throwing stuff.

Interesting to note that while they were doing the refurb, the entrance on Ashton Lane had to be moved slightly to comply with building regulations. Not much though - it was *"just a jump to the left"*...

The Ashoka was (and still is) one of the best curry houses in Glasgow. It was at the top end of the student budget, but well worth pushing the (gravy) boat out for. The choice was fabulous and I'm pretty sure I had something different every time I went. It never disappointed.

Back Alley Burgers was located across Byres Road in Ruthven Lane and did no nonsense cheap burgers for students. Ruthven Lane was also home to *Di Maggio's* which opened its doors in 1985 and was the location of my first date with Mrs McL.

The *University Café* served up mouthwatering 'multi-item' breakfast rolls and amazing Italian ice-cream which was much better than *Mr Whippy* (or *Mr Bunny* or *Mr Softy* for that matter).

Chimmy Chunga's was directly across the road from *Clatty's* on Great Western Road and was one of the first big Mexican restaurants to open in the West End. Shortly after its opened its doors, Billy Connolly put forward the idea that Mexican food is essentially all the same, the only difference is how it's folded. Whilst this is not strictly accurate, you should never let the truth get in the way of a good story.

This was all pre *McDonald's* remember, so if you fancied a quarter pounder with cheese you were stuck with *Wimpy* or *Casey Jones* at Central Station. *Wimpy* got acquired by *Burger King* in 1989 which was probably for the best…

Arran

CHAPTER ELEVEN

ARRAN

Our family has had a small holiday home in Whiting Bay since 1972 which my mum still lives in today.

We had started visiting Arran as a family in the late sixties, initially staying in Lamlash before moving five miles down the coast to what would become our island retreat for the next fifty years.

We spent all our school holidays and nearly every weekend at our house in Sandbraes, and so it genuinely felt like I had grown up in both places. My mum & dad moved there permanently in the late eighties, by which point my sister had married an

Arran farmer and had settled on the island with a growing brood.

Arran is quite often described as '*Scotland in miniature*' as it showcases everything people love about the Scottish countryside. Mountains, lochs, rivers, forests & beaches. It's absolutely stunning. Many people got their first Arran experience via a school geography field trip only to return later in life with their own families and friends to enjoy the enormous range of outdoor activities like: kayaking, paddleboarding, mountain biking, canoeing, gorge walking, rock climbing, orienteering, horse riding, hillwalking, cycling and of course golf.

There are seven golf courses on the island which is a massive number for such a relatively small place. Three of them are full size 18-holers, two are 9-hole affairs and there's also one 12-hole course and one with just 11. So it's no real surprise that this is where I learned to play golf in the early eighties.

Prior to that, pretty much the only thing I did was fish. I would disappear for entire days and then return at night with my oilskin jacket pockets stuffed with brown trout (and the occasional sea trout). It had one of those Velcro flap front pouches which on my way out in the morning would contain a handful of worms from the garden and a sandwich. When I got back would be home to God knows what. I think in hindsight it might have been a subconscious way of breeding maggots for bait.

I remember people thinking it slightly odd that I always wore my oilskin even if it was a roasting hot day. To be fair, they had a point. I suspect I only did it as I felt I needed the pocket capacity.

We lived a hop and a skip from the beach in Sandbraes and had a small fibreglass dinghy which we used for sea fishing trips in the bay. It even had a name made up of the first two letters of each of our names: 'FIANDO'. On flat calm summer days we would head out into the bay and bring home boat loads of mackerel which we would smoke over wood chips and turn into pâté which would then be spread over toasted plain bread (yes the kind that came in the tartan waxed paper). It was delightful, and provided you with at least a year's worth of your omega-3 recommended allowance. I'm actually quite surprised that *John West* didn't try to acquire us.

When I wasn't fishing I would often head off birdwatching with my mum. We had some fairly memorable spots including a goldcrest (Europe's smallest bird) and some golden eagles (which are one of the largest). Between us we ticked off a pretty impressive number over the years as Arran's island micro-climate meant you got some fairly unusual visitors (and some fairly unusual birds too). I clearly took it all in at the time as I'm still able to get a few pointless answers when the bird questions come up. In fact, I would seriously consider choosing British birds as my specialist subject if the BBC were ever stupid enough to allow me on *Mastermind*.

However I swapped my fishing rod for a five-iron in the early eighties and quickly developed a healthy-ish obsession with golf. Whiting Bay was a relatively short course with nine par 3s and nine par 4s, but it had the kind of Himalayan landscape that gave you a proper cardio workout.

Most of the holes had fairly tiny greens which meant you had to be seriously accurate with your approach play. It would be fair to say that I didn't always quite manage that and I remember once over clubbing my shot into a neighbouring garden. It was a fairly new ball so I decided to climb over the fence to retrieve it whilst failing to spot the garden rake as I landed. I ended up getting a hole-in-one, and a big bruise on the other one.

Although the tight perimeters of the course resulted in you losing lots of balls, it also meant you could find a lot too, so I would head out on to the course with a poly bag most evenings to replenish my supply.

Some of the richest pickings were to be had on the left of the 15th fairway where if you hit even a slight draw with your tee shot, there was no hope of retrieving your ball as there was a big ravine with a fast-flowing burn at the bottom of it.

So I stupidly thought this would be the perfect place to look, completely oblivious to that fact that not even Edmund Hillary would have thought about venturing down there without the aid of a safety net and a sherpa. I should have known better.

Although it was a nice warm sunny afternoon, I had conveniently ignored the fact that it had been raining for the previous few days and so although the surface seemed fairly dry, the stuff underneath it definitely wasn't.

As I'd suspected, there were hunners of top quality balls to be had, so I started filling my empty *Woolworths* bag and began to congratulate myself on having had such a brilliant idea. But it wasn't a great time to lose your concentration.

It's a horrible feeling to realise you're sliding down a grassy slope with no ability to stop before you reach the edge. Fortunately, I landed squarely on my right ankle which pretty much exploded on impact. If it had been any other part of my lanky teenage frame I probably wouldn't have survived. So escaping with just a compound fracture of the tibia & fibula plus a bump to the head was really quite astonishing.

When I eventually came round I managed to shout loudly enough for someone to spot me and raise the alarm so that the Arran Fire & Ambulance Service could do their thing.

However while we were waiting for them to arrive, a couple of people had walked up the burn from a safe spot to give me a bit of first aid. One of them spotted the (now) half-empty poly bag and the substantial quantity of grade-A golf balls scattered around. He kindly suggested that he would 'look after them for me'. I don't think he ever had to buy a new golf ball again. Bastard.

However in a quite remarkable stroke of luck, one of the most respected orthopaedic surgeons in the country just happened to be working at the Arran War Memorial Hospital and he did an outstanding job of putting humpty dumpty together again.

Other than having two months off school (and a very big stookie), I ended up being none the worse for my wee tumble. The only lasting memento was being left with one leg slightly shorter than the other which ironically helped me navigate the undulating Arran terrain much better than I used to.

I also discovered years later that my 'before and after' X-rays had featured in one of the respected medical journals of the time to illustrate what was possible with a steady hand and a *Meccano* set.

Although most of my golf was played at Whiting Bay, our most enjoyable rounds as a family fourball have been on the twelve-hole course at Shiskine with Corrie coming a close second.

The scenery at both these spots is spectacular and epitomises why Arran becomes such a special place for so many of us.

In the 1980s, the Whiting Bay Clubhouse would turn into a lively social space in the summer evenings and that was probably one of the things that got me into performing music. There was always someone there with a guitar and a humorous song or two - often brilliantly improvised to suit the audience of the night. I remember thinking I'd quite like to do that.

From the mid to the late 80s I was part of a folk band who used to perform in some of the Arran bars during the peak season. I guess it was 'semi-professional' as we got paid, however we invariably drank it all before we left the venue.

I remember *The Blues Brothers* out-drinking their fee at *Bob's Country Bunker* after pretending they were the *Good Ole Boys* by performing the theme tune from '*Rawhide*' and '*Stand by Your Man*' by Tammy Wynette. The gig paid $200 but the band ended up drinking $300 worth of beer. To be fair we were never quite that bad. We also played more than two types of music (as opposed to just *country & western*). But we probably only played three types to be fair.

Prior to us hitting the big time, my Saturday nights in Arran would have been spent at the discos either at Nags in Whiting Bay or in the Brodick Hall where the legendary *Tiger Tim* would occasionally make an appearance. But once I'd got the gigging bug there was no going back (...and I was a shite dancer anyway).

Cutting our teeth performing at the Douglas Hotel and the Cameronia Bar was certainly character building and meant that from then on we all had the confidence to get the party started pretty much anywhere.

***

Now perhaps I have a selective memory, but the ferry journeys to and from Arran in the eighties just seemed to be so much more straightforward than they are today. Sure, we had some stormy crossings occasionally but the ferry always seemed to sail even if it was a bit of a bumpy ride. In fact, I remember being thrown around the ship quite a few times but we just found it hilarious and weren't in the least bit bothered.

So it's a real shame that the chronic disruption to the ferry service in recent years has had such an impact on the local island community. Wouldn't it be good if they finally did something about that?

TONGS YA BASS!!
buckfast

CHAPTER TWELVE

TONGS YA BASS

There exists an entire generation of Glaswegians who will pick up a food serving implement and feel compelled to say: *"Tongs Ya Bass"*. Despite how it sounds, it's actually one of the warmest greetings you can exchange. Graffiti really meant something in those days…

Despite its traditionally rough reputation, Glasgow has never taken itself too seriously and the long established tradition of ensuring there is always a traffic cone on the Duke of Wellington's napper is a perfect visual representation of that. I remember the local *Evening Times* newspaper having a front page headline which read: *"MAN WANTED FOR ARMED ROBBERY"*. The following morning they received more than 200 applications.

We also have an amazing talent for expressive use of language. For example in Scotland there are more than 70 words for drunk. A bit like Eskimos having 50+ words for snow I suppose. Here are just some of my favourites:

- Pished
- Sozzled
- Blootered
- Hammered
- Steamin'
- Fleein'
- Stocious
- Rubber
- Aff yer coupon
- Mangled
- Sloshed
- Slabbered
- Mingin'
- Oot the game

I think the reason I like this selection is because they are all quite onomatopoeic and evoke wonderfully visual representations of what Glaswegians think drunkenness looks like. I'd love to find out what the Eskimoan word is for *blootered.*

I studied maths and can clearly remember one of the fundamentals of multiplication & division is that two negatives make a positive. However in Glasgow, two positives can actually make a negative. The most obvious example being *'Aye right'* - which clearly means anything but. And is there any other language in the world where (phonetically) you can repeat the same word three times in quick succession to indicate the location of something?

"Excuse me big yin - where are the Mortons rolls?"
[Me pointing] *"There they're there".*

However there is one Glasgowism which is my absolute favourite. I'll start with a bit of context just to set the scene for any non-native speakers. In Scottish Fish & Chip shops, a main item plus chips is called a *supper* (e.g. a fish supper = fish + chips).

If you want just a main item without chips, it's called a single (e.g. a single fish) …which also means something else in Glasgow rhyming slang but I went for one earlier…

So on that basis, a single black pudding is a black pudding without any chips. Easy enough to grasp (quite literally). But sadly this all starts to break down when it comes to sausages. One sausage plus chips is called a sausage supper. However normal Scottish chip shop sausages (as opposed to German sausages - or '*saveloys*' if you live in Kelvinside) are not actually that big which means that most people who choose sausage as their chip companion would opt for a *double sausage supper* which is two modestly sized sausages plus chips. Which is fine - unless you wanted a reasonably sized portion of sausage but no chips, which results in the factually accurate (but slightly confusing) order of a '*single double sausage*'.

I should stress at this point that most people in Glasgow would completely understand what a '*single double sausage*' was and so there would be no risk of embarrassment (unless of course you wanted to have two portions).

We will deep fry most things like hamburgers, half-pizzas, pies, haggis etc. however despite its near legendary status, I don't think I've ever seen a *deep fried mars bar* gracing a Glasgow chip shop menu. But I have seen quite a few deep fried *Cadbury crème eggs* and some absolutely enormous fritters. No wonder we have a life expectancy of forty-three…

Anyway, where was I? Oh yes, the slightly unusual but entirely explainable Glasgow sayings. Again this is just a small selection of my favourites:

Gaun yersel

Go for it! I have complete confidence in you.

That would gie you the boak

That would have the effect of making you sick.

Ya dancer!

A moment of celebration, success or triumph.

Gie it laldy

Put in as much effort & enthusiasm as you can.

Yer bum's oot the windae

You're talking pish/you've left yourself in a foolishly exposed position.

Ma heid's mince

My brain is struggling to cope with everything.

Yer yer maw's spit

There's quite a strong maternal family resemblance.

That's pure bowfin'

Gosh, that's a particularly offensive smell.

That's a pure riddy by the way

That must have been very embarrassing for you.

Did ye, aye?

I'm not convinced what you're saying is true.

I can see it far enough

I'd prefer not to do that particular thing.

...good luck with all that *Duolingo*!

Glasgow also developed its own variety of rhyming slang which was much more tongue in cheek than its cockney counterpart. Two of the more interesting things about Glasgow rhyming slang are:

(a) The word it's rhyming with is often already a slang word in its own right.

(b) You're not actually required to say the second word in a couplet.

A couple of examples of the latter might be:

"I'm just going for a *Greyfriars*" or
"Do you fancy popping out for a few *Salvadors*?"

I'll leave you to work these out while I go for a quick *Lillian*...

One of my other favourites (often heard the morning after a big sesh) is: "Here, let me pour your tea. Looks like you've got the Hatties*

[**Hatties**: The *Hattie Jacques* = the shakes]

We're also pretty good at inventing our own words for things, often removing the need to have multiple words when one will do:

Bahookie

Your buttocks/bottom/bum/backside.

Toley

A wee jobby (often resembling a *Malteser*).

Sheuch

The little gap at the top of your bahookie cleft where a bead of sweat can sometimes gather.

Stoater

Something that's extremely good/excellent. Can also be used in its adjective form: *Stoatin'*.

Fanny

A bit of an idiot (but in an affectionate way). For example your mum might say to you "Don't be such a fanny", or perhaps in a group situation "Don't do that, we'll look like a bunch of fannies".

There's one final example which I think captures Glasgow's personality perfectly.

Cyndi Lauper was a pioneering pop rebel with colourful hair and a wacky wardrobe. So I guess she was a kind of singing *Vivienne Westwood*. She burst on to the scene in the early 80s with chart topping hits like Girls Just Want to Have Fun and Time After Time. Anyway, her surname sounds like the perfect description of how your head feels the morning after a few too many swallies (as long as you pronounce it 'Laʊ/per').

'Ma heid's loupin' is a well-established way of describing that intense, throbbing headache that makes you want to hide under the covers for weeks. I'm sure many of us have shown our true colours by waking up on New Year's Day with a massive *Cyndi.*

THE NORWEGIANS

CHAPTER THIRTEEN

THE NORWEGIANS

I have a long and happy association with Norway. I'm fortunate to have got to know lots of fantastic Norwegians, many of whom are all still close friends forty years later.

We met at Glasgow University where they studied things like computing and engineering. So they were clever guys and most of them were also very tall & handsome (which had its benefits). The majority of them had done a year of national service in the military prior to coming here, so they seemed like good guys to hang around with. They also got fairly generous government loans to study abroad and a significant number of them chose to come to Glasgow. The student's union became a very natural gathering place for them and the beer bar was much the richer for it (quite literally).

They were great fun to be with and blended in seamlessly with the Glasgow culture. In fact, they became adopted Scots in 'jig time' and we even had a Norwegian president of the Union in 1990.

They made the absolute most of their time in Scotland and explored the countryside during their weekends, resulting in them becoming vastly more knowledgeable than any of us locals.

Some of them were quite big. One of my pals was 6 ft 9 and another was an Olympic shot putter, so they were exactly the kind of guys you wanted to be hanging around with in Glasgow on a Saturday night. Sadly, both of them left us too soon and are much missed.

There is a close cultural bond between Scots and Norwegians which I guess makes sense as the Vikings spent a fair bit of time raping and pillaging us in the ninth century. But hey, let bygones be bygones and all that. To be fair, it was quite a while ago, and nowadays we seem to have a much more closely aligned outlook on life. Similar latitude, similar attitude and a surprisingly similar language. In fact, many Norwegian words are remarkably close to their Scottish equivalent:

- *Hus* = house (hoose)
- *Mus* = mouse (moose)
- *Barn* = child (bairn)
- *Bra* = good (braw)
- *Ut* = out (oot)
- *Rumpe* = rump/bottom (bahookie)
- *Velkjent* = well known (well kent)

There's a lower league Scottish football team called Stenhousemuir which almost certainly derives from the Norwegian term *Sten Hus Mur* which translates as 'Stone House Wall'. This is probably why 'The Warriors' have such an unusually large Norwegian following. In fact at home games, almost 50% of the fans are from Norway. Unfortunately that's about 12.

I discovered early on that Norwegians make jokes about the Swedes. What I also discovered was that most of the jokes the Scots would traditionally make about the English/Irish/Welsh also appear in the Norwegian national joke book. In fact the *Norsk gutta* claim that they originally came up with all of these treasured comedy nuggets and that the Scots had subsequently stolen them. Aye right!

I remember my first trip to Norway in 1988 which included a five day stay in a cabin deep in the Norwegian mountains. One of my friend's families owned a summer house in Rjukan, a stunning forest setting but with no electricity and no running water. Undeterred, I packed my fishing equipment and got on the plane looking forward to experiencing the Scandinavian wilderness.

When I landed safely in Oslo, the Norwegian passport control guy spotted my rod & reel said "Ah, fisketur? (fishing trip?) I replied "Nei, drikketur (No, a drinking holiday) which raised a smile from him. If only all immigration officers were so friendly!

When we got to our wooden hut, the lack of mod cons meant we lived off beer and hot dogs*. We had a small camping stove to cook the sausages on and chilled our beers in the nearby stream.

* *Pølse med lompe* is a delicious savoury snack consisting of a (single) hot dog sausage wrapped in a big flat potato scone tortilla. It's a very popular after-the-pub nosh option for Norwegians so I guess it's their equivalent of a kebab (but just a bit healthier and much less messy).

The one thing that struck me when I visited Norway for the first time was just how clean it was. There was no litter and they clearly took great pride in keeping the place in good order. One way of achieving this was to offer a refundable deposit on all glass bottles which was a huge incentive. You got 1 NOK back per bottle (around 9p) and after our forest retreat we managed to return around (ahem) 500 bottles and got the equivalent of 45 quid which we spent on a very welcome and necessary sit-in Chinese meal on our way back to Oslo. The food was excellent but the highlight was using the hot towels to have our first wash in nearly a week.

We also went for a swim in *Tinnsjøen* which is the third deepest lake in Europe and featured in the 1965 movie '*The Heroes of Telemark*' starring Richard Harris and Kirk Douglas. It was fucking freezing.

***

Jahn Teigen is infamous for being the first act in modern *Eurovision Song Contest* history to score zero. *"Norvège nul points"* ("Norway, no points"). But Jahn had the last laugh as his non-scoring song *Mil Etter Mil* (Mile After Mile) spent months at the top of the Norwegian charts and made him a bloody fortune.

After becoming a bit of a folk hero, he went on to represent Norway on two further occasions (1982 & 1983) where he fared considerably better finishing in 12th and 9th place respectively. Well done Jahn for sticking with it. The only way is up!

Shortly after Jahn hung up his microphone, Norwegian pop music hit new heights when *A-ha* burst onto the scene in the mid-eighties. It then became even cooler to hang around with Norwegian guys as they all looked and sounded like Morten Harket. However aside from Scandinavia's synth-pop sensation, I'd started to discover that Norwegian drinking songs were also exceptionally good. Lots of animated actions and table thumping with a pretty impressive amount of drinking involved.

I really liked the one which was based around the months of the year. The basic premise was that if you were born in the particular month featured in that verse, you had to finish your drink in a one-er. For example: *Om så født i januar* (if you were born in January), put your glass to your mouth and drink. The last verse roughly translated to 'anyone who was ever born at all' (i.e. in any month of the year) was required to 'down it in one'. Anyway the inevitable result of all this nonsense was that the whole place got absolutely hammered.

***

Once we'd finished university and gone our separate ways, our close friendships continued. This was partly due to some of the guys marrying Scottish girls, but also thanks to twenty-two of us investing in some Islay single malt whisky. We bought a sherry cask of *Bruichladdich* and 16 years later had it bottled and got just over a dozen each. As a cask strength spirit, it needed to be handled with care as at 58% proof it could easily have resulted in a lost weekend.

For nearly two decades it gave us a brilliant excuse to get together every couple of years on Islay to check in on our investment and have a taste. As 'owners' we got the full red-carpet treatment and the distillery made us all feel incredibly special. The cask that we purchased was originally a 400 bottle barrel, however over nearly twenty years, the *angel's share* reduced it down to just under 300. But still a fabulous return on our original investment although it was never about the money. It was all about an enduring bond between two countries who shared so much, including an almost identically sized population and lots of trees.

***

Hägar the Horrible was a fictional Viking from a small coastal village in Norway. He appeared as a comic strip in *The Sun* for many years and he was also the cheery, hairy face of *SKOL* beer adverts on TV. He was created by the American cartoonist Dik Browne and was around from the early seventies until the late 80s. Interestingly, the comic strip also appeared in Norway, however the protagonist's name in the Scandinavian version was *Hårek den Hardbalne* which (with a bit of poetic licence) translates to '*The Hairy Guy with Hard Balls*'.

***

I spent my sixtieth birthday cruising the Norwegian fjords which was simply wonderful. The scenery was breathtaking and more than two thirds of our voyage was spent within the Arctic Circle so the sun never actually set. In fact on the night of my birthday we stood out on the rear deck at 2am in broad daylight and watched a pod of minke whales give us a special private performance. It truly was a fantastic day and it's no exaggeration to say that the north of Norway feels like heaven.

Fun fact: We began our trip just a few kilometres from the Russian border in a small town called *Kirkenes* which is actually further east than Istanbul. It just goes to show what a huge country Norway is and how scarily close it is to the former Soviet Union.

Sweet Dreams
(Are Made of This)
TOFFOS
Chewy Toffee
Barratt
SHERBET
DIP
DAB
Birds Eye
ARCTIC ROLL
TUNNOCK'S
TUNNOCK'S
TEA CAKES
Birds
Angel
DELIGHT
FIZZY LIZZY
CHEW BAR

CHAPTER FOURTEEN

SWEET DREAMS

(ARE MADE OF THIS)

Scotland holds a pretty impressive number of world records, however one of the more notable ones is for cramming the maximum possible amount of sugar into a single molar wrecking treat. The two most infamous examples being *Tablet* and *Macaroon Bars*.

Even the sweetest teeth struggled to cope with the sheer sugariness of these delicacies. *Coconut Ice* was also well over the legal limit for the sweet stuff.

We are also the current holders of the record for the confectionary with the greatest ability to pull out teeth and fillings simultaneously. The legendary

McCowan's Highland Toffee bar. Their factory was in Stenhousemuir and so presumably lots of travelling Norwegian football supporters would end up going home with their mouths glued shut. We also had *Lucky Tatties* but nobody really knew why...

However there is one brand that will forever define Scotland's love of sugar and that's *Tunnocks.* You can now find *Tea Cakes, Snowballs, Caramel Logs* and *Caramel Wafers* all over the world (although the *Snowballs* are usually squashed).

Thomas Tunnock was a teacake trailblazer and way ahead of his time. He started the business in 1890, but it was the 1950s that saw the arrival of the iconic delights that we know and love today. It was yet another great example of Scottish innovation as it was just after the war when sugar was still being rationed which drove the need to create products with longer shelf lives.

We lived in Uddingston in the 90s and always felt a sense of pride when we saw the red foil on our travels. Even now, the Tunnock family are more than capable of leading me into temptation. We even had dancing teacakes at the opening ceremony for the

Commonwealth Games which just goes to show the level of love that people have for the Lanarkshire luxuries.

At least a quarter of my school mates were from Italian families and the vibrant Tuscan community in Glasgow helped ensure that we were blessed with some truly excellent *gelato.*

My two favourites were *The University Café* on Byres Road and *Queens Café* on Victoria Road (not to be confused with *The Queens Park Café* which we've already established is a boozer). We also had Equi's, Coia's, Crolla's, Jaconelli's, Valerio's in Muirend, and of course Nardini's which has always provided an excellent excuse to stop off in Largs on your way to Millport. I also have fond memories of Pellegrini's in Brodick. Their enduring success just goes to prove that in Scotland it's never too cold for ice-cream.

Although a trip to the local ice-cream shop was always a real treat, many of us got our pokey hat fix via them coming to us. The tuneful jingle of the van's imminent arrival would induce an almost Pavlovian response. This was mostly because people loved their sweet frozen desserts, however many of the vans also sold some slightly more addictive stuff (shocking I know…)

The ice cream wars got a brief mention in the movie chapter, however it probably deserves a bit more coverage as it was a pretty big deal in the 1980s. But I think it's best that I leave that to the 'Serious Chimes Squad'.

I prefer to use the melodious mobile cone dispensaries as an opportunity for more jokes:

[Man with very raspy sore throat]
Can I have a 99 please?
[Ice Cream van vendor] *Crushed nuts?*
[Man with sore throat] *No, laryngitis.*

[Customer] *Can I have an ice cream please*
[Vendor] *Hundreds & Thousands?*
[Customer] *No, just one thanks.*

So having established that the people of Greater Glasgow have an unhealthy fondness for sugar, the *Alpine* Lorry expanded its geographic coverage to incorporate central Scotland. They had a much wider selection of flavours than any of the other fizzy pop providers and they quickly realised they were on to a winner. We felt like the kids in America!

The main thing I recall was that their *Limeade* was incredibly green, almost fluorescent in fact. They also did *Pineappleade* and *Cherryade* but the top seller was always *American Cream Soda*. I'm surprised they weren't banned sooner, as those bottles contained more E-numbers than an explosion in a *tooty frootie* factory.

Talking of *tooty frooties*, we should really have a quick wander back down the confectionary aisle. As someone with a very sweet tooth, or to be more accurate about 31 of them*, I feel suitably qualified to talk about some of the more memorable offerings of the era.

*(*Should really be 32 however I have a partially erupted lower back left wisdom tooth so I don't feel I can legitimately count that one).*

I'm somewhat ashamed to say that I've enjoyed all of these 80s sweetie legends on more than one occasion:

Toffos

Available in plain, mint & assorted.

Texan bars

One of the chewiest things you could ever imagine. So chewy that it was virtually impossible to have a sensible conversation until about an hour later.

5-4-3-2-1

*M*uch of its success was due to its terrifically catchy Manfred Mann TV ad tune. The *'five treats in one'* consisted of: milk chocolate, crispy rice, caramel, wafer, and fondant. This particular confection was introduced in 1980 and then discontinued in 1989 so it was probably one of the very few genuine '1980s' treats.

Dairy Crunch

Milk chocolate & crispy rice, so equal to exactly 2/5ths [or 40%] of a *5-4-3-2-1.*

Cabana

Basically a *Bounty* with sliced cherries inside.

Wham Bar

Introduced in the eighties but still available today. You would often see the young guns go for it. Made by the highland toffee people from Stenhousemuir.

Mint Cracknel

Sounds like a menthol Olympic rowing champion but it was actually an extremely enjoyable crunchy, layered minty, crystalline treat covered in rich milk chocolate which splintered when you ate it.

MB Bars

Also known as Monster Bars. Famous for being the only chocolate bars that weren't wrapped. A bit like a slightly stale *Fry's Chocolate Cream* in the scud.

Sherbert Dip Dab

A wee red lollipop that you dipped into fizzy sherbet powder and then made a horrible mess of yourself.

Spangles

Square boiled sweets in a variety of exciting flavours (particularly in the 'Old English' packs).

Drifter

Caramel/wafer-based chocolate twin bar. An idea that was almost certainly stolen from Tunnocks.

Caramac

A bit like eating a tin of brown condensed milk.

Rowntree's Secret

Basically a long rectangular walnut whip with a kind of bird's nest outer shell.

Spanish Gold

Sweet pretend tobacco strands. Why?

Golden Cup

Milk chocolate segments filled with a rich liquid caramel. It was almost too sweet but the texture contrast was marvellous.

Bar Six

Segmented chocolate bar with wafer and hazelnut cream. Most often found in swimming pool vending machines.

Banjo

Never thought I'd be 'picking' that one! Phased out in the mid 80s as despite it sticking up 'two fingers' at *Twix* and the *Drifter*, it was never quite as good.

Fizzy Lizzy

A chewy sweet filled with sherbet that was so zingy it would make you pull a funny face. Another stoater from Stenhousemuir.

Sweet Cigarettes

I know - what were we thinking in those days?

Old Jamaica

Rich rum & raisin dark chocolate from the Caribbean (but made in Birmingham).

Five **Centres**

Who can forget the pure excitement of not knowing what colour/flavour you would get next! However occasionally the different fondant colours weren't completely aligned with the ridged divisions in the chocolate, so you would get sneaky peek…

Anglo Bubbly

Been around forever but most prevalent during the 80s. Almost impossible to remove from clothes/faces etc. You can still find lots of it under that bridge near Central Station.

Hubba Bubba

A more refined bubble gum offering which didn't stick to your coupon.

Nowadays we have access to some much higher quality confectionary and it's really quite annoying to be at an age where I should be cutting down on sugar. But hey - life's too short, and I still often find myself looking for Lindor.

***

AN ERA OF CONVENIENCE

It's no exaggeration to say that in the 1980s we ate a load of shite. As if the sweeties and fizzy drinks weren't bad enough, we were also subjected to:

Findus Crispy Pancakes

Always golden brown but occasionally a bit floppy. Contained various types of molten lava.

***Pop* Tarts**

A similarly lethal scalding hazard but with a sweet jammy filling.

Pot Noodle

Instant carby snack in a variety of synthetic plasticky flavours.

Micro Chips

What microwaves were invented for. Always best to opt for the crinkle cut version to maximise ketchup coverage.

Primula Cheese Spread

A staple for your house party buffets as you could just squeeze it onto *Ritz Crackers* and voila! - you had a kind of cheap Glasgow *vol-au-vent.* It had a large star shaped nozzle which meant you could do artistic piping.

Arctic Roll

Quite possibly the most popular dessert of the decade despite it tasting like frozen carpet.

Angel Delight

One of the two titans of the whiskable dessert market and the arch-rival of *Instant Whip.*

Instant Whip

The nemesis of *Angel Delight* which I have to say I preferred as their Butterscotch flavour was sugarier.

Dream Topping

Subtly different to the other two as it was just a topping. However it had a really catchy ad song so it probably sold more than it should have.

Viennetta

This means nothing to me! (thanks Midge - I'll buy you an ice-cream)

Sunny Delight

Ridiculously over-sweetened OJ.

It's no wonder that so many of my school friends went on to become dentists. They'd clearly worked out that they were sitting on a bloody goldmine. In fact I'm sure they couldn't wipe the smiles off their *Happy Faces*...

HOGMANAY HIGH JINKS!
Ok Stirlin'....
oot the car!
POLICE
THE
FAMOUS
GROUSE
SCOTCH WHISKY

CHAPTER FIFTEEN

HOGMANAY HIGH JINKS

New Year's Eve is a big thing in Scotland. So big in fact that we get an extra day's holiday to recover. Apparently the reason is that Scottish people used to work during Christmas and therefore felt the need to properly go for it the following week. I'm not sure I buy that as although it might be factually correct, I think we just like any old excuse for a big party.

Traditionally Hogmanay would turn into a three day bender which started with an afternoon liver acclimatisation warm-up session followed by a brief scran-stop enroute to a huge ceilidh followed by some first footing involving coal, shortbread and lots of supermarket bought whisky. Then on New Year's Day you would have a hangover-curing steak pie lunch washed down with a gin & Irn Bru chaser followed by a brief afternoon snooze before finding a suitably gatecrashable party in the evening. Our additional day's public holiday on January 2nd would typically consist of defibrillation, a brief fight with the family and an unsuccessful attempt to remember whose couch you slept on.

For those who were slightly more culturally adventurous, the *Edinburgh Street Party* came along in the early 90s and is now universally recognised as one of the greatest outdoor celebrations of New Year's Eve in the world. It begins with a torchlight procession and culminates in a spectacular firework display above Edinburgh Castle, with some brilliant live music stuffed in the middle. In 1996, more than 300,000 people turned up on the night which resulted in a much more rigorous ticketing approach which now limits the crowds to more like 50,000.

But back in the 80s things were much simpler. You just turned up at your friend's house with a half bottle of *Famous Grouse* and hoped for the best.

However the weather can be pretty brutal up here, so nowadays most Scots just choose to curl up in front of a roaring spouse and watch the whole thing unfold on TV. It certainly beats waiting for a non-existent taxi in the freezing cold knowing that the only thing you're likely to get into is a fight.

If there was one thing guaranteed to keep people in front of the TV on Hogmanay, it was *Scotch & Wry*. Rikki Fulton was a comedy genius.

His gloomy *Reverend I M Jolly* monologues became an unmissable part of the year end calendar as he had an almost unnatural ability to sound like a thoroughly miserable old bastard. However it was his opening *Supercop* sketches which set the tone for what we knew would be yet another unforgettable Hogmanay TV memory:

"OK Stirlin' oot the car"

...followed by his goggles pinging over the back of his crash helmet. You knew it was coming, but you still weren't able to stifle the inevitable giggle which followed.

Every sketch was a comedy nugget and my favourite has to be the one where he wakes up on New Year's morning with his head on the kitchen table nursing the hangover from hell. He starts reading a letter from America sent by his sister and says to his wife:

[Rikki] *Is that an 'o' or an 'a'?*
[Wife} *I think it's an 'a'.*
[Rikki] *Thank God for that, I thought my brother-in-law had shot himself...*

There were many other Scotch & Wry classics like the appallingly unhygienic chef *Dickie Dandruff* preparing one of Scotland's less well-known national delicacies - *The Sheep's Heid.* He demonstrated one of the critical aspects of the dish which was to marinate it in just the right amount of white wine: "*aboot a moothful an a hauf*".

Another of the more colourful characters was *Aloysius McGlinchey* - the gallus Glaswegian with the most acute case of malapropism ever witnessed. His *magnum opus* was his appearance in court after being charged with throwing a mutton pie at a Partick Thistle football player. He chose to conduct his own defence which was a piece of comedy perfection. He opened by suggesting that we all need to keep things in 'Perspex' and claimed that he was nothing more than a 'victim of circumcision'. He was determined not to be incarcerated again and end up like the 'Birdman of Alka-Seltzer'.

After this stoatingly eloquent summing up, he was acquitted by the judge at which point Mrs. McGlinchey shouted "Aw ya beauty!" and Aloysius chimed in with "Cry freedom ya bass!"

The Curries was a marvellous parody of *The Corries* (who wrote our national anthem). Roy and Ronnie were Scottish folk singing heroes but nobody was safe from Rikki's wicked wit. The sketch was centred around a gorily gruesome ballad about the Glencoe massacre resulting in one of them getting the boak. The bearded collie (sorry Corrie) began by setting the scene:

"It was a brutal time when brother butchered brother and men hacked bits off other men. When soldiers with dirty

great long swords disembowelled other soldiers whose swords wurnae quite as long. It was a time when rivers ran wi' blood and oozing entrails stained the heather"

...and cue the non-bearded Corrie dry boaking. The chorus went like this:

- *They grabbed his heid and severed it, and then ripped oot his tongue,*
- *It wriggled like a jellied eel on the grun where it was flung,*
- *They beat his brain to a throbbin' mush and slashed his guts asunder,*
- *Then cut his heart oot with a dirk, and he died. Nae bloody wonder!*

The ballad was cheerily entitled: *"The Splattered Blood of our Slaughtered Sons"* and was only slightly more horrific than the original *"Massacre of Glencoe"* song that the Corries had subjected us to.

To be fair, Ronnie & Roy also sang a much less gory tune about *Bonnie Prince Charlie* escaping on a boat to Skye dressed up as a woman after watching his army get humped at Culloden. However what the song failed to mention was that oor Charlie was about as Scottish as a plate of spaghetti bolognese.

But sadly, *Scotch & Wry* was pretty much the only good thing about Scottish television on New Year's Eve, as the 'official' Hogmanay shows in the 1980s were pretty awful. The main culprit was STV who flitted between their gaudy hay-baled studio ceilidh format and some excruciatingly appalling experimental efforts. The kitschy hoedowns were hosted by the *Laird O' Coocaddens,* Jack McLaughlin (no relation I'm relieved to say).

Jack did a terrific job of reinforcing Scottish stereotypes by depicting us all as a bunch of teuchter pensioners lapping up a cheesy cocktail of tasteless tartan tackiness, foreboding folk songs and some very camp dancing. However, any port in a storm I suppose and we ended up watching it anyway as the only alternative was to talk to your family.

Occasionally the shows would include acts that were almost impossible to describe - like the catastrophic Coatbridge caricatures, *Fran & Anna.* They would appear in tartan mini-dresses, rouged cheeks and matching tartan hats with feathers on them. However the Watt sisters were probably two of the nicest people in showbiz and were the epitome of the heather & haggis approach to Scottish light entertainment. They very cleverly fed off the ribbing they got from *The Laird* and used it to propel their careers to the point where they became a regular fixture on the *Terry Wogan* chat show in the 1980s.

The STV Hogmanay programmes would also feature overused comedians like Andy Cameron and Allan Stewart whose humour was so inappropriate that it's embarrassing even thinking about it. One year they even had Russ Abbott on the Hogmanay show dressed as Jimmy McJimmy (yes, that's what I thought). However normal-ish service was resumed when Sydney Devine appeared in his pale grey *Farah* stay-press action slacks to yodel us into 1986.

But to be fair, the STV production team were acutely aware of the public perception of their 1980s shows and were happy to adopt a self-deprecating approach to creating something new (ish).

Things started to improve in the early nineties when the BBC finally presented us with something a bit more representative of what the viewing public actually wanted. It became a much more balanced mix of contemporary pop and musical Scottishness, courtesy of Phil Cunningham's accordion and Aly Bain's fiddle.

The warm-up acts for the Hogmanay Live shows also saw a massive improvement during the 1990s with *"Only an Excuse?"* kicking off in 1993 and *"Chewin' the Fat"* in 1999 (the latter giving birth to *Still Game*).

***

Having acknowledged that New Year is traditionally a bigger celebration in Scotland than Christmas, it's important we don't forget that we do a pretty good job of delivering on the previous week's festivities. Scotland does Christmas as well as anyone however I've always been a bit perplexed by some of the bizarre yuletide rituals that we continue to observe:

- Why do we get drawn into trying to outdo our neighbours with our external lighting displays?

- Why is it that we feel compelled to drink a load of obscure out-of-date booze that we wouldn't normally even use for unblocking the sink?

- Why do we spend hours & hours trying to choose the perfect gift just so that the recipient can spend twice as long queueing to take it back?

- Why do people think it's ok to start interfering in the Christmas dinner prep after a few too many Buck's Fizzes? Too many cooks spoil the broth. Too many pished cooks spoil the whole fucking meal.

- And finally, why do we think it's acceptable to slurp trifle out of the fridge at 3am? For me, that will always remain a sweet little mystery…

GETTING OLD

CHAPTER SIXTEEN

GETTING OLD

Any of us who spent our early adult years in the 1980s are now approaching sixty (if we haven't got there already). So I feel I should acknowledge some of the significant and uncomfortable changes that brings. However before we get into that, I wanted to rewind a bit to the first time it struck me that I was probably well past the halfway mark…

On my fiftieth birthday, I received a kind and thoughtful present from NHS Scotland. A jobby kit. I guess many of us are familiar with the NHS bowel cancer screening program, however I thought it was worth sharing some of the more interesting details.

At that time it was called the Faecal Occult Blood test (FOB) however it's since been upgraded to the Faecal Immunochemical Test (FIT). The original FOB version was a bit more fiddly but the general principle was much the same.

My initial test had come back positive (and so had the second), so my prize was a free, all-inclusive trip to the colonoscopy department (complete with fairly hideous preparation procedure).

Interestingly, part of the prep involved going through two days of a low fibre diet. Yes, a *low* fibre diet. Fortunately Glasgow is one of the few places in the world where that's even possible. The list of approved foods resembles what you might expect to get on a *Scottish Scurvy Society* outing to Saltcoats. It's actually fairly difficult to find food without any fibre in it but with a little bit of research you can create a reassuringly traditional Scottish menu including nostalgic staples like gammon steak, fried eggs and a Glasgow salad (chips).

The final 24 hours of prep is a solid free affair and involves four litres of liquid laxative. It's pretty difficult to drink four litres of anything, however this stuff is vile. I presume there's some sort of complex mathematical algorithm which can determine the correlation between how dreadful something tastes and how effective it is at doing its job. All I can say is that this stuff certainly did its job for me.

So having survived the preamble, I turned up for my colonoscopy procedure and waited my turn. They do a kind of 'on the day prioritisation' exercise based on age/weight/general health/how scared you look etc, so I was actually quite pleased to be put near the back of the queue as I guessed that meant I was considered to be a low risk contestant. The procedure wasn't actually too bad, just a little bit uncomfortable and embarrassing. During the show, you are put under 'conscious sedation' so you can watch the whole thing unfold on the big screen if you like. They pump lots of air into your bahookie, which can make for very amusing results - particularly if like me, you grew up in the whoopee cushion era. (Note: I always felt that *Whoopee Goldberg* should have married *Peter Cushing*).

Anyway - while they're up there, they get the secateurs out and do a bit of light pruning to remove anything that shouldn't be there, and the whole thing is over and done with in about twenty minutes.

Once you're finished, you get wheeled off to the recovery area for an hour before you're allowed home. Now I've always been a fan of a bit of toilet humour, but this stuff was on another level. Because you've had gallons of air pumped into your colon, after a while it feels a fairly pressing need to make its way back out again. However the marvellous thing is that because your intestine has been completely evacuated, you get the brass band without the 'brass neck' (i.e. a completely odourless performance.)

The nursing staff on the ward were brilliant. They basically said fill your boots and offered a prize for the loudest one (…which I think was a kite).

The recovery ward could easily have secured a slot at *Last Night of the Proms*. I'm convinced I heard the final 'movement' from *Mozart's Horn Concerto No.4 in E-flat major*, followed by the iconic raspy sax intro from Gerry Rafferty's 'Baker Street.'

But let's get back to the present and the trials and tribulations of entering your sixth decade…

There's nothing funny about lying prostrate with your prostate pressing up against your (ahem) Glasgow area. It inevitably results in you having to make multiple visits to the toilet during the night. But it happens to all of us, and as long as we set some simple rules we can minimise any disturbance to our bed partner. One request that your other half might make is: Don't wake me up before you go-go because if you do-do this could be our last Christmas.

Somebody once said: *"You know old age is starting when you struggle to bend over without risking farting."* This is worryingly accurate. I can remember Billy Connolly observing that once you hit fifty, it's almost impossible to get in and out of your chair without making 'involuntary noises'.

So if you've started to notice something in the air tonight then there's your answer. You might think it's just a careless whisper but you can never be too sure. Which reminds me of the story about the old lady in the nursing home saying to one of the staff: *"I think I've just done a silent fart. What should I do?"* The kind and considerate carer replied: *"I think you should replace the batteries in your hearing aids".*

I know that my ability to remember 80s song lyrics now exceeds my ability to remember why I've just gone upstairs. However on a positive note, I've discovered that I can now get to Oban on the bus for a pound without having to do any busking. However most of the changes I'm starting to notice are a little bit more worrying - for example:

- Breaking into what you think is a run when in fact it's just a slightly more animated walk with no actual increase in speed.

- Going for an exciting trip to the supermarket and then spending the rest of your day trying to remember where you parked the car.

- Finding hair growing in unusual places (like your ears, nose and the back of your neck). What on earth is all that about? I remember Sean Connery being rightfully proud to show off his magnificent carpeted chest back in the day, however at this stage in my life any form of body hair is just a bloody nuisance.

- Starting to prioritise practicality over fashion by buying things like *Clarks* wide-fit, rip tape *velcro* strap loafers with dual-density footbed and *permagrip* soles. I just hope to God I never buy a belted anorak.

- Creating complex mathematical models to try and work out how many 'non-jiggered' years you have left and whether it might make sense to 'front-load' the pension budget and splurge it on opulent cruises to the Galapagos Islands. (However I'm conscious it might just be me that does this).

But perhaps the most profound and dramatic change we go through is developing an almost pathological obsession with stayin' alive. We start to have deep and meaningful conversations with our GPs about last-minute life elongation strategies by asking them questions like:

"If I reduce my drinking, cut out fatty foods and eat less sugar will I end up living longer?"

Now there are typically two answers to this question:

(a) No, it'll just feel like it.
(b) We'll not know until somebody's tried it.

The other one I like is the story about the man who goes to see the doctor about his toilet habits. He tells him that he has a bowel movement at 7am every morning. The doctor tells him that's great to hear as it's important to stay regular at his age. The man explains that the problem is that he doesn't actually get out of bed until eight o'clock.

So on that basis, is it really such a big deal to try and hang around in this life for as long as you can? Billy Connolly was almost certainly correct when he said that although clean living might buy you a few more additional years, that period of extra-time comes at the very end of the game when you're unlikely to be able to find the ball (never mind kick it).

Old age comes to us all, but the bit I fear the most is the arrival of the walk-in bath and the motorised stairlift. My anxiety is related to the fact that I've never quite worked out how walk-in baths work as the only options I can see are:

(a) You get in with it empty and then fill it up which means that you either risk scalding yourself or catching a chill in the Trossachs …or

(b) You fill it up first and then check that the temperature is suitable before opening the door and then watching in disbelief as the water cascades down the stairs drenching your beloved spouse as they come up on the stairlift.

I'm under no illusions that I've started to slide down the slippery sudoku-solving slope to senility. But it's important to focus on the positives. I'm very much alive & kicking and I know I'll always be young at heart. All I would ask is that I'm able to retain my dignity (…I should be so lucky!)

But despite how I've made it sound, getting old isn't so bad as the older we get, the more stuff we have to look back on and cherish.

The 1980s was an amazing decade to grow up in especially if you lived in Glasgow. I have so many special memories that I'll take with me into my own final chapter and I'll always be incredibly grateful for that.

Glasgow - do I love you?

Yes, I love you.

*****

AFTER WORDS

This is my first book and against all odds I've been able to complete it without having to resort to the sledgehammer. In fact it's been my favourite waste of time and I'm pleased to say that I'm still standing.

However, occasionally it's been a thorn in my side but luckily I haven't had to rip it up and start again (and that's really saying something).

My fabulous wife has been extremely patient while I stay up all night long (all night) finishing yet another chapter. She's also made lots of very helpful suggestions (although I'm not sure I can print any of them). I wouldn't go as far as to say that every little thing she does is magic, but she does have a high tolerance threshold for my idiosyncratic gibberish, especially when I get into the groove. I would often disappear for hours on end and she would politely ask, "Is there something I should know?"

I would say of course not darling - I'm your man, I'm crazy for you and I'm never gonna give you up. Just leave me to it and I'll get it finished (knowing that left to my own devices I probably would).

You've got to have faith and realise that when the going gets tough it's just one moment in time. Sometimes it's felt a bit like the never ending story and it's taken so long that my hair is starting to fade to grey. But there's no point putting yourself under pressure. Although it's been a labour of love, I never wanted to kiss this thing goodbye, as I just couldn't imagine spending my remaining years wishing I was lucky.

ACKNOWLEDGEMENTS

My biggest thanks go to my wife for putting up with my ridiculous nonsense for thirty-five plus years. I remember sharing my initial ideas for the book as we drove down though Skye after getting stormbound on North Uist on our anniversary. You reassured me that it was worth doing and you've supported me all the way. I love you lots.

To my mum Aileen. Knowing that you have your mother's unconditional love makes everything in life so much easier. Thanks Mum. Hopefully some of the memories in the book will raise a smile in Whiting Bay. I apologise for the odd sweary-word appearing here and there but to be fair I have tried to limit it as much as I can. I'll claim poetic licence for the ones that stayed.

Our two sons, Ciaran & Dec. You spent your formative years having to listen to my terrible puns and even terribler dad jokes. Thanks for laughing at them (even if they weren't actually that funny). I love you and I'm very proud of both of you.

My late dad for helping me fill up my early joke books and for creating the opportunity for us to perform together as the *Folkal Chords* in Arran during the eighties.

To my older sister Fiona and my big brother Angus. It can't have been easy to have an attention seeking 'wee' brother (although to be fair I'm the tallest). You've always embraced my wacky songs & even wackier jokes, particularly the ones you had heard lots of times before. We all need to do our bit to help the environment and my small contribution has been to recycle my material.

To my fabulous friends, and especially those who I spent most of my time with in the eighties. The memories we created together are very precious and have helped generate most of the subject matter for this book. So thanks for providing all of the content free of charge. I love you all.

And to my English teacher Ronnie Renton. Although I was always more of a maths guy, I still remember your *figures of speech* lessons like they were yesterday. So I hope you like my artistically adept and admirably abundant application of alliteration.

And lastly to all of you for buying and reading my first book (or being regifted it by someone who doesn't really like you).

Thank you. It means a lot.

Donald x

APPENDIX: THE SONGS

This is where you get to mark your own homework. As I said at the start, I've made my definition of the 1980s slightly more elastic so that I can include a few tracks that felt like eighties songs even though they were actually released in the late 70s or early 90s.

Here are the **170**. Hope you scored well!

SONG/ARTIST	YEAR	PAGE
Tinseltown in the Rain The Blue Nile	1984	3
Play the Game Queen	1980	5
Jump Van Halen	1984	5
Hunting High and Low A-ha	1985	5

Song / Artist	Year	
True		
Spandau Ballet	1983	5
Just an Illusion		
Imagination	1982	12
Making Your Mind Up		
Bucks Fizz	1981	12
Land of Make Believe		
Bucks Fizz	1981	12
The Look of Love		
ABC	1982	14
Perfect Skin		
Lloyd Cole and the Commotions	1984	15
Too Shy		
Kajagoogoo	1983	15
Love and Pride		
King	1984	15
RELAX		
Frankie Goes to Hollywood	1983	16
Two Tribes		
Frankie Goes to Hollywood	1984	17
I Want Your Sex		
George Michael	1987	17
Like a Virgin		
Madonna	1984	17

Like a Prayer		
Madonna	1989	17
Mad World		
Tears for Fears	1982	17
I Want to Break Free		
Queen	1984	17
Planet Earth		
Duran Duran	1981	17
Love of the Common People		
Paul Young	1983	17
Goody Two Shoes		
Adam and the Ants	1982	18
Physical		
Olivia Newton-John	1981	18
The Power of Love		
Frankie Goes to Hollywood	1984	18
The Power of Love		
Jennifer Rush	1984	18
The Power of Love		
Huey Lewis and the News	1985	18
Don't Let the Sun Go Down on Me		
George Michael	1985	20
Do They Know it's Christmas		
Band Aid	1984	22

We Are the World
USA for Africa 1985 22

Return to Innocence
Enigma 1993 24

Teenage Kicks
The Undertones 1978 28

Walk Like an Egyptian
The Bangles 1986 28

Funkytown
Lipps Inc 1980 30

Waterfront
Simple Minds 1983 30

Some Guys Have All the Luck
Rod Stewart 1984 32

Dance Yourself Dizzy
Liquid Gold 1980 34

Drive
The Cars 1984 34

Magic
Olivia Newton-John 1980 35

Going Underground
The Jam 1980 36

West End Girls
Pet Shop Boys 1984 36

Never Can Say Goodbye
The Communards 1987 37

Bad
Michael Jackson 1987 43

Holiday
Madonna 1983 44

It's a Sin
Pet Shop Boys 1987 48

Sunshine on Leith
The Proclaimers 1988 50

Just Can't Get Enough
Depeche Mode 1981 58

Freedom
George Michael 1990 58

Flash
Queen 1980 60

Dancing with Tears in My Eyes
Ultravox 1984 62

My Camera Never Lies
Bucks Fizz 1982 62

The Whole of the Moon
The Waterboys 1985 62

Flashdance...What a Feeling
Irene Cara 1983 62

It's a Kind of Magic		
Queen	1986	63
Another Day in Paradise		
Phil Collins	1989	68
Respectable		
Mel and Kim	1987	69
Suddenly		
Billy Ocean	1985	71
Come on Eileen		
Dexy's Midnight Runners	1982	71
So Lonely		
The Police	1978	71
Only When you Leave		
Spandau Ballet	1984	72
I'm Gonna Be (500 Miles)		
The Proclaimers	1988	72
Nothing Ever Happens		
Del Amitri	1989	72
Money for Nothing		
Dire Straits	1985	72
19		
Paul Hardcastle	1985	73
Cruel Summer		
Bananarama	1983	73

Song / Artist	Year	Page
Synchronicity I The Police	1983	74
Desire U2	1988	77
Every Breath You Take The Police	1983	84
Truly Lionel Richie	1982	87
The Final Countdown Europe	1986	88
Sign of the Times The Belle Stars	1983	89
Start The Jam	1980	94
Shaddap You Face Joe Dolce Music Theatre	1981	97
Vienna Ultravox	1981	97
Embarrassment Madness	1980	98
Save Your Love Renée and Renato	1982	98
The Bucket of Water Song The Four Bucketeers	1980	98

Snooker Loopy		
Chas & Dave and the Matchroom Mob	1988	98
Snot Rap		
Kenny Everett	1983	98
Chalk Dust - The Umpire Strikes Back		
The Brat	1982	98
Arhtur Daley E's Alright		
The Firm	1982	99
Star Trekkin'		
The Firm	1987	99
Eat It		
Weird Al Yankovic	1984	99
Beat It		
Michael Jackson	1982	99
N-N-Nineteen Not Out		
The Commentators	1985	99
Ullo John! Gotta New Motor?		
Alexei Sayle	1984	99
The Chicken Song		
Spitting Image	1986	99
Agadoo		
Black Lace	1984	99
The Sun Always Shines on TV		
A-ha	1985	100

Video Killed the Radio Star		
The Buggles	1979	100
Jackie Wilson Said		
Dexy's Midnight Runners	1982	108
To Cut a Long Story Short		
Spandau Ballet	1980	109
Just What I Always Wanted		
Mari Wilson	1982	112
Loch Lomond		
Runrig	1983	112
Back to Life		
Soul II Soul	1989	114
I Could Be Happy		
Altered Images	1981	126
Cars		
Gary Numan	1979	120
Always on My Mind		
Pet Shop Boys	1987	137
Alone		
Heart	1987	137
Hungry Like the Wolf		
Duran Duran	1982	139
Senses Working Overtime		
XTC	1982	139

Tempted		
Squeeze	1981	139
Imagine (re-release)		
John Lennon	1981	141
Patience of Angels		
Eddi Reader	1994	142
One Vision		
Queen	1985	142
Perfect		
Fairground Attraction	1988	155
Oblivious		
Aztec Camera	1983	155
I Should Have Known Better		
Jim Diamond	1984	155
Shout		
Tears for Fears	1984	156
Wouldn't It Be Good		
Nik Kershaw	1984	160
Words		
F. R. David	1982	170
Sometimes		
Erasure	1986	170
Girls Just Want to Have Fun		
Cindi Lauper	1983	171

Time After Time		
Cindi Lauper	1983	171
True Colours		
Cindi Lauper	1986	171
New Year's Day		
U2	1983	171
Electricity		
Orchestral Manoeuvres in the Dark	1980	178
Pride (In the Name of Love)		
U2	1984	179
The Only Way Is Up		
Yazz and the Plastic Population	1988	180
Lost Weekend		
Lloyd Cole and the Commotions	1985	181
Fantastic Day		
Haircut 100	1982	183
(Feels Like) Heaven		
Fiction Factory	1984	183
Sweet Dreams (are Made of This)		
Eurythmics	1983	187
Temptation		
Heaven 17	1983	188
Kids in America		
Kim Wilde	1981	191

Song / Artist	Year	Page
Young Guns (Go for It)		
Wham!	1982	193
Gold		
Spandau Ballet	1983	194
Looking for Linda		
Hue and Cry	1988	196
Golden Brown		
The Stranglers	1982	197
Letter from America		
The Proclaimers	1987	206
1999		
Prince	1982	211
Celebration		
Kool & the Gang	1980	211
Sweet Little Mystery		
Wet Wet Wet	1987	212
Over and Done With		
The Proclaimers	1987	218
Baker Street		
Gerry Rafferty	1978	218
Wake Me Up Before You Go-Go		
Wham!	1984	219
Last Christmas		
Wham!	1984	219

In the Air Tonight
Phil Collins 1981 219

Careless Whisper
George Michael 1984 219

Lady
Kenny Rogers 1980 219

Stayin' Alive
The Bee Gees 1977 221

Alive & Kicking
Simple Minds 1985 223

Young at Heart
The Bluebells 1984 223

Dignity
Deacon Blue 1987 223

I Should Be So Lucky
Kylie Minogue 1987 223

Cherish
Kool & the Gang 1985 223

Against All Odds
Phil Collins 1984 225

Sledgehammer
Peter Gabriel 1986 225

My Favourite Waste of Time
Owen Paul 1986 225

I'm Still Standing
Elton John 1983 225

Thorn in My Side
Eurythmics 1986 225

Rip It Up
Orange Juice 1983 225

Really Saying Something
Bananarama with Fun Boy Three 1982 225

All Night Long (All Night)
Lionel Richie 1983 225

Every Little Thing She Does Is Magic
The Police 1981 225

Into The Groove
Madonna 1985 225

Is There Something I Should Know?
Duran Duran 1983 225

I'm Your Man
Wham! 1985 226

Crazy For You
Madonna 1985 226

Never Gonna Give You Up
Rick Astley 1987 226

Left to My Own Devices
Pet Shop Boys 1988 226

Faith
George Michael 1987 226

When the Going Gets Tough
Billy Ocean 1985 226

One Moment In Time
Whitney Houston 1988 226

Never Ending Story
Limahl 1984 226

Fade to Grey
Visage 1980 226

Under Pressure
Queen & David Bowie 1981 226

Labour of Love
Hue and Cry 1987 226

Kiss
Prince 1986 226

Kiss This Thing Goodbye
Del Amitri 1989 226

Wishing I Was Lucky
Wet Wet Wet 1987 226

Catterglen Publishing

www.ingramcontent.com/pod-product-compliance
Lightning Source LLC
Chambersburg PA
CBHW032002050726
47590CB00006B/2017

* 9 7 8 1 9 1 9 4 8 5 8 0 5 *